ALONG THE MEKONG

Along the Mekong

Fast and Slow Boats
Through Cambodia and Laos

MARCO CARNOVALE

Other books by Marco Carnovale

Al di là del Muro: Avventure di un Maggiolone Giallo al di là della Cortina di Ferro, 2020

Beyond the Wall: Adventures of a Yellow Volkswagen Beetle on the other side of the Iron Curtain, 2018

Viaggio alle Maldive: Una non guida di viaggio per svelare le isole, 2017

Journey to the Maldives: Unveiling the Islands of an Archipelago on the Brink, 2015

European Security Institutions after the end of the Cold War, 1994

The Control of NATO Nuclear Weapons in Europe, 1993

La Guerra di Bosnia: Una Tragedia Annunciata, 1992

Soviet-East European Relations: Continuity and Change, 1989

All books are available on Amazon

or contact the author at **carno.polo@gmail.com**

To Lifang, the love of my life

Contents

List of Images

PREFACE

*B*uddha did not leave any of his wisdom in writing, but he is reported to have said that luck happens when opportunity meets preparedness. There is no such thing as fate, or chance.

It was on a sunny day in the early spring of 2002 that I decided to travel to Cambodia and Laos. It was a difficult moment for me, and it was not fun at that time, but I later would be grateful for it. I did not look for either the setbacks or the opportunities that presented themselves to me that year, but I am happy I was mentally prepared. That Spring turned out to be a pivotal moment when I took decisions that would shape the rest of my life.

I was emerging from a professionally challenging period in my life. After a stint at NATO Headquarters, working as a political officer, I had been offered what looked like a dream job as deputy director of an American foundation. In fact, at the same time, I was also offered another great job teaching at an American university, but declined it. I was enthusiastic and put all my mind and my heart into the new challenge.

It could have been an exciting new page in my professional life but things did not work out as expected, the dream became a nightmare and I left the foundation after a few months. In the meantime the university had hired someone else. To make matters worse, I also broke up with my girlfriend.

I was alone and out of a job.

Of course, I started looking for another job, though not really for another girlfriend. However, while I was sending out CVs, I decided to take a "gap year," the sort of thing people do in their early twenties, though I was in my early forties. But I needed some fresh air. So I *concluded it was time to start traveling full-time, for some time, maybe for a long time. Time, suddenly, acquired a whole new meaning. I would be able to send CVs and search the internet for jobs from anywhere in the world. The world wide web was still in its infancy but I could sit at any internet café on the planet and look for suitable vacancies. In-person interviews would have to wait.*

I had already traveled a lot by then, of course, but mostly to easy destinations, staying in comfortable accommodations. I wanted to rough it a bit, try and dig deeper into some countries that had always interested me. It was at this moment that my life-long friend Roberto said he was about to lead an adventure tour to Indochina.

I had never been to that region, though I had long been interested. I once wanted to volunteer as an undergrad at Georgetown to work in Red Cross camps in Thailand, where refugees from Cambodia who managed to escape the Khmer Rouge were housed and fed. But I was not accepted. Having grown up in the seventies I was, of course, keenly aware of the Vietnam war and its collateral conflicts in Cambodia and Laos. Also, I had specialized in communist countries when doing my Ph.D. at MIT in the eighties, and Indochina had plenty of those. I immediately decided to join Roberto's party.

In May 2002 Roberto and I sat down with a large map on his office desk and went over the itinerary. The plan was to move mostly by boat, motoring upstream the great river and stopping at various places along the way, some of which would be world renown sites and others much less so. We would start from Bangkok, the great hub of South East Asia, from which it is almost obligatory to start a trip to Cambodia and Laos. We would then fly to Siem Reap (Angkor) and from there use various boats, big and small, fast and slow, to travel to Phnom Penh, and then on to Kratie and Stung Treng.

Next would be a border crossing into Laos at the Don Khon waterfall of the Mekong; then continue to Pakse, the current capital Vientiane, the old capital Luang Prabang and then up Mekong's tributary, the Nam Ou river, until Muang Khua. We would at that point have to see what the local road situation would be in this time of heavy monsoon rains, but would try to move on overland to reach the northernmost tribal areas of Laos, near the border with China.

We had a plan, and started to count down the days.

Acknowledgements

Many people helped me experience this journey and without them this book would not exist. First of all I would like to thank the hundreds of Cambodians and Laotians I met, who were always open to share their life with me even if we hardly ever shared a common language. Special thanks to go Somlit, our Laotian guide, who led us through the tricky paths of the jungle and made sure we saw as much as possible and stayed out of trouble.

I would also like to thank my fellow travelers Mario, Maria Vittoria, Renata, Paola, Luca, Barbara for having shared the fun, their views, their impressions of what we saw and their constructive spirit. My thoughts also go to Loredano, the jovial dentist from Liguria who, no matter what, loved to sit down and eat his proper daily hot lunch, and who sadly passed away a couple of years ago while on another adventure tour. Finally, I would especially like to thank Roberto, who led our small group of adventurers, for having shown me a new way to travel. After our trip to Indochina I actually followed his footsteps and became an adventure tour leader myself, traveling off the beaten track around the world for the next ten years.

The trip narrated in this book turned out to be a milestone in my life, so that my "gap year" first morphed into a "gap decade", and then became a permanent lifestyle.

Confucius said we only have two lives: the second begins when we realize we only have one. This trip was the beginning of my second life.

No more sending CVs around, I only accepted occasional consulting jobs and founded a club in Brussels, organizing events related to adventure travel and the world's cultures. I was having fun like never before, meeting the most interesting people who ever crossed my path and even making some money out of it.

Indochina further developed my interest in east Asia and this led me to meet the love of my life a few years later, and I am now married to an elegant, smart and beautiful Chinese lady. I could not be happier.

Throughout the book the reader will find, interspersed between chapters and sections, reviews of books (and one film) that helped me understand better what I saw during my trip. Some of these I read before traveling, some after returning home, hard to say which was more useful. Most books are in English but I added a few in Italian as well. The text in italics is taken from the various books' own back covers or online descriptions, while the following review in normal text is my own.

Kraainem, May 2021

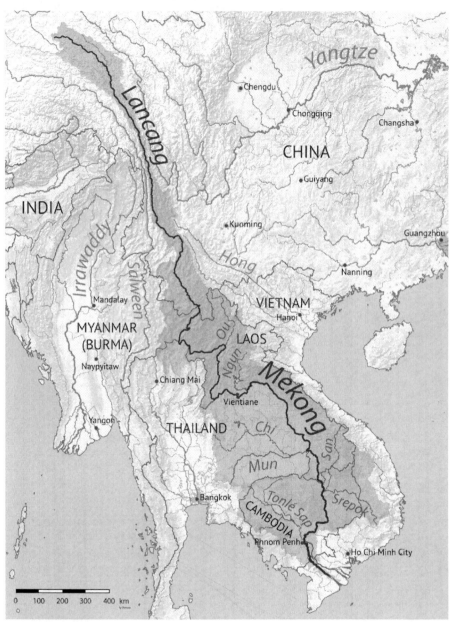

1. The Mekong River and its main affluents © Shannon1 CC

1. INTRODUCTION: HOW AND WHY

I traveled to Indochina in August 2002, on a Swiss airplane from Zurich. I had flown with them on numerous occasions, but never had they been so courteous as on this flight; it must have been their fear that, after Swissair's bankruptcy, the face-lifted "Swiss" airline (same planes, same livery, same crews, the Swiss were not so creative this time) was their last chance to survive.

Off to the East

Yet, the plane, a beat-up Boeing 747, was old and noisy and I was not sure about the future of this airline... but I was flying in business class for free on my long accumulated frequent flyer miles so I could not really complain, could I? I tried to rest after a meal of which I recall an excellent salmon and a moderately long and complex Burgundy chardonnay, but could not really fall asleep. So I started thinking about the trip ahead, and about the meaning of it all, in terms of the countries I would visit and the moment in my life when this was happening.

Ever since I was an adolescent I had become convinced that travel was an indispensable tool for a well rounded upbringing. I simply assumed that confronting my Italian ways with those of other peoples would allow me to compare and contrast different value-systems and educational methods and then to improve on my own. My main intellectual challenge in high-school then became that of finding a way to prepare for a future career that would allow me to travel and know the world. After considering a variety of possibilities I applied to and was accepted at the School of Foreign Service of Georgetown University, in

Washington, DC and chose to major in international politics. Soon after I arrived there in 1978 I first became interested in South East Asia.

The Vietnam War era student protests were over, but one could still witness their reverberations on campus. I once saw former Secretary of State Henry Kissinger, perhaps the main architect of the US strategy in South East Asia, being loudly booed by my fellow students while trying to deliver a foreign policy lecture.

In Indochina itself, the final rounds of the war were still being played out: four years after the humiliating American departure and the collapse of the corrupt regimes they had backed in Saigon (today's Ho Chi Minh City), Phnom Penh and Vientiane, the Vietnamese had firmly established their military influence over Cambodia and Laos. Yet, as it often happens at the end of wars, things were not going well for the victors, and a human tragedy of biblical proportions was in the making. Vietnam was now a united country, and the communist North was supposed to have liberated the corrupt capitalist South. One big happy nation again. If only...

In fact, hundreds of thousands of Vietnamese from the defeated Republic of South Vietnam became knows as the "Boat People". They tried to escape misery and persecution by the communist regime by boarding whatever vessel they could get themselves on to, seaworthy or not, and sailing away, often without either a destination or adequate skills, instrumentation and supplies for a sea voyage; many died doing so, either drowning in storms or victims of pirates. Countries from around the world sent ships to rescue the Boat People.

It was on this occasion that my own country, Italy, for the first time after World War II sent armed forces on a national mission away from home territory. After photographs by the famous journalist Tiziano Terzani made Italians aware of the tragedy that was unfolding in the South China Sea, the government decided to deploy the navy to try and rescue at least some refugees.

Three naval ships, destroyers *Andrea Doria* and *Vittorio Veneto* and tanker *Stromboli*, left Italy in July 1979 and reached Indochina a couple of weeks later. They immediately ran into all kinds of boats loaded with refugees. Through an interpreter who had been taken along from Italy, this is the message that was read out loud to the Vietnamese: *"The ships near you belong to the Italian Navy and have come here to help you. If you wish so, you can embark them as political refugees and be carried to Italy. However, beware that the ships can only take you to Italy, but they shall neither carry you to other nations, nor tow your boats. If you do not want to board, you can immediately receive water, food, and health care. Tell us what you want to do and what you need."*

In 45 days the ships explored 75.000 square nautical miles, took on board 902 desperate Boat People who were screaming from their rickety vessels and brought them back to Italy. This was a small number when compared to the hundreds of thousands Vietnamese who took to sea and did not survive. The exodus continued for years. The last Boat People set sail in the mid-1990s.

The Vietnamese Boat People were not the only refugees escaping the "peace" which followed the American withdrawal: perhaps even more dramatic was the tragedy of the Cambodians who fled from fighting and famine in the aftermath of the Vietnamese intervention in their country on Christmas Day in 1978. Within a month the invaders had deposed the odious Khmer Rouge Regime of Pol Pot that had been in power since 1975 and was responsible for the killing of up to two million out of a total 1975 population of six and a half million; in relative terms, the worst genocide in modern history. The situation in the country was desperate, the economy was a complete and utter shambles, the Vietnamese had taken Phnom Penh but Pol Pot's forces still held vast areas in the North and in the West of the country and continued to fight. Exile seemed to most to be the only hope.

Refugees streamed out of Laos as well. Several hundred thousands were estimated to have crossed the Mekong into Thailand after the Communist victory in 1975. Many of them, but not all, belonged to the Hmong ethnic group of northern Laos, who feared retribution because they had fought on the side of the pro-US government against the Communist Pathet Lao and the North Vietnamese. Many other Laotians simply ran for their dear life. Laos, officially neutral in the Indochina war, had first been infiltrated by North Vietnamese forces who established the "Ho Chi Minh Trail" through the Laotian (and Cambodian) jungle to resupply the Viet Cong guerrilla in South Vietnam.

In a clumsy, cruel and ultimately futile attempt to interrupt the flow of men and weapons along the "Ho Chi Minh Trail", the United States ran a decade-long secret (because Laos was neutral) bombing campaign which failed in its mission but caused untold suffering among the civilian population. It gave Laos the dubious distinction of being the most heavily bombed country in history – more bombs were dropped on it than were used against Germany during the entire World War II. The bombing obliterated scores of villages and left behind a landscape strewn of unexploded ordnance which represents a major hazard to this day, as do the land mines were laid indiscriminately in the millions by all sides.

Most of these Cambodian, Laotian and Vietnamese refugees had sought protection in Thailand. They had been accommodated in refugee camps on their way to third countries, usually Europe or the United

States. I had followed these events as closely as possible – which, under the circumstances in the country, was not very close at all. Georgetown had offered its students the possibility to work as volunteers in these camps in Thailand and offered to give a semester of academic credits for those who did. I applied but was not selected. I was disappointed, but by now my mind was set on spending a semester abroad, doing some field work, and as I had developed a certain skeptical curiosity for Communist countries I ended up instead spending the spring of 1980 in Poland. That was in itself a formative adventure, and I have written about it in my book "Beyond the Wall: Adventures of a Yellow Volkswagen Beetle".

Which was just as well as this was the time of the build-up to the strikes of Gdansk of August 1980 which would catapult Lech Wałesa onto the international scene and initiate the process of dissolution of the communist regimes in Eastern Europe. My stay in Poland was the beginning of a career as political scientist and international civil servant which kept me focussed on European affairs and transatlantic relations, and thus away from South East Asia.

However, I continued to follow events there – wwhich became relatively easier after the economic (but not political) opening of Vietnam, Laos and Cambodia in the late eighties and especially in the nineties of the XX century.

Why travel?

As I mentioned earlier, in 2002 I had decided to make traveling my full-time occupation for the foreseeable future, so I spent many hours asking myself why. Usually I would have a "why" ready by the time I made an important, life-changing decision, but this time I did not. I had not planned it, I did not know where it would lead me and was not sure it would work. But I had decided, I was making a clean break, so I wanted an explanation.

Usually, scientists elaborate a hypothesis on paper, and if it works in theory they then move to the laboratory and test whether it works in practice. My plan would work in practice, I was reasonably sure, so all I had to do was to investigate whether it would work in theory. Or put it another way, I knew how I would organize my lifestyle in the coming years, but I did not know why.

As I munched some Brazilian nuts while the Swiss stewardess mixed my *Bloody Mary*, I came to realize that I believed a journey was like a work of art: it should ideally be either enjoyable or interesting – and preferably both. But if traveling was neither enjoyable nor interesting, why bother? Better stay home, unless one was forced to travel unwillingly by some sort of *force majeure*, like business, natural calamities or war.

If a work of art neither appeals to aesthetic taste, nor conveys any message, the viewer probably will not remember it for long, and will not make an effort to go see it again. On the other hand, if a work of art is considered by a viewer to be beautiful, he or she might wish to buy it if that is an option, or to see it again in a museum, even if it does not carry any particular message with it. Likewise, if a work of art is not really beautiful, but does convey a philosophical, religious, political or any other type of message, it will be worthwhile to study it, maybe buy it, and anyway retain it in our memory and go back to it for future reference.

Much in the same way, travel makes sense if it gives pleasure to the traveler (or explorer, or tourist, I will not get into what is the difference between them here) even if one does not learn much – say a trip to Disneyland. However, travel might be just as worthwhile, and arguably more so, if one learns from it, even if it means going to places which are not especially beautiful or enjoyable to visit – say a tour of a war zone.

In an ideal journey, in my view, one would both enjoy beauty and find interest. My journey to Cambodia and Laos, which constitutes the object of this book, definitely falls into this third category of travel. These countries host world class natural splendors and sophisticated cultural and artistic traditions. But they also reveal many patterns and problems of modern development, some of which are unique, while others might be applicable to other developing countries around the world.

There are three categories of people who choose to travel to distant, exotic, and often poor places like Cambodia and Laos. Each has perfectly legitimate reasons to travel and it is not my intention to criticize any of them. It might be useful, however, to describe these different approaches.

The first group I would call the country collectors. Though they may not admit it, they go to these countries with the same mental attitude they have when visiting an exhibit, a zoo, or Disneyland. They are curious, but not really interested. They hear the sounds of a country, but do not listen; the see the sights, but do not really look carefully at much.

They like ticking countries off their checklist, one year in Laos, the next in Guatemala, then on to Central Africa. They enjoy traveling but have no real drive to even begin to understand. At most, they will go on some shopping spree, to bring home the modern equivalent of the trophies of old, such as some fine cloth or funny clothes, a cute artifact or possibly some piece of antiquity which is often all the more exciting as it is usually forbidden to take it out of the country.

There is nothing wrong per se with this group though they may not be my most interested readers. I hope some will buy my book and get something out of it. I would love nothing more, of course, than to be proven wrong here! Well, perhaps they can pass it on to some of their friends who belong to one of the two other groups!

The second group is made up of what I would call the eternal romantics. They like distant, mysterious places almost by definition, before even setting foot on their soil. This is especially true of poor countries where subsistence agriculture is a major component of the economy. When they get there, they fall in love with almost everything they see, and tend to blame any obvious problem they witness (poverty, illiteracy, disease, etc.) either on past colonial rule or on current World Bank driven and inevitably ill-conceived development projects, ruthless western big-business greed, male-dominated globalizing influences – or on all of the above.

Ah! if only these people had been left alone to mind their own business and live life at their own pace, they way they had always done it, how much better off they would be, the romantics think. When they see an illiterate child playing in the mud, or an open sewer in a malaria infested jungle village, they think it is sooooo beautiful, take a picture, perhaps dispense a pen or a candy here and there, try to establish some sort of communication to prove the happiness of their interlocutors and move on. When they see an ox-driven plow their eyes brighten, it is something they instinctively think is good, genuine, authentic, traditional and that should be preserved. By contrast, when they see a tractor, their shoulders drop in resignation, this is the local culture and civilization being spoilt by careless western interference, and being lost forever.

The eternal romantics tend to see the glass always half empty, and fear that, as history keeps drinking at it, it will soon be completely empty. They are at heart conservatives (though few would accept to characterize themselves as such, except perhaps in the strictly environmental sense of conserving nature), their main desire being to slow down the pace of change, to preserve anything that is old and traditional, no matter what. Yet, something, anything, is not good and worth preserving just because it is old. And it is not necessarily beautiful, either. They built bad stuff in antiquity too.

The eternal romantics would rather see a developing country sealed off to foreign trade, inestment, advice and tourism than being influenced – they would say "spoiled" – by any of them. They always regret that after opening to the outside world the country in question will never be the same again. In this, of course, they are right, it won't. The question is: will it be better off or worse off? The eternal romantics assume the latter, but they do not always have a strong case.

In reality, idealizing the past and hoping it will come back is just not good enough, especially in developing countries. In the history of western civilizations, romantics have produced great literature and art, but rarely useful policy-oriented ideas, and I fear the same applies when present day romantic travelers. Again, there is nothing wrong with romantics except for the fact that they are much better at nostalgically regretting or recriminating than they can ever be at proposing better alternatives to the reality they do not approve of. Because of this attitude, eternal romantics are often unable to enjoy travel, as they more often than not suffer at seeing the places they visit losing their old "true" nature and acquiring new, foreign traits.

I would call the third group of travelers the modernizers. They see the glass as half full and think history is always pouring more water to fill it up but are never satisfied that it does so fast enough. Modernizers are usually critical of the status quo they witness in the countries they visit – as well as what they leave behind in their own. They see international contacts, be they scientific, economic, political, or at the personal level, as a way to exchange experiences and improve everyone's lot. They see international tourism playing an important role in these exchanges as one of several ways in which countries can benefit from knowing each other a bit better.

The problem with the modernizers is that, as they work for their ultimate goal of open international communication, they often pay too little attention to where each individual countries is starting from and what specific circumstances might require their balanced development not to emulate the experience of others but to acquire tailor-made approaches of their own. Like the eternal romantics, but for opposite reasons, the modernizers are rarely pleased with the half-full glass, and as a result suffer during their travel at what they perceive to be an endless string of missed opportunities for improvement.

The aim of this book is to tell the story of that journey as I saw it through my eyes of eclectic traveller, critical political scientist and avid photographer. I will try to convey both what was beautiful and what was interesting.

I hope this book will appeal to the eternal romantics as well as to the modernizers. Both groups might find stimulus for further developing their own thoughts. I do not expect these readers to agree with all of my impressions and assessments. Indeed, I would be worried to hear that anyone does. I will have been successful if during this virtual trip through to the last page the reader is stimulated to share some of my enjoyment, to think through some of the issues I raise, to do some additional reading and, most importantly, to travel to Cambodia and Laos.

As a political scientist, I have learned to beware of situations in which everyone agrees. Free thinking, the basis for democracy (which Winston Churchill brilliantly characterized as the worst political system in the world except all the others) needs civilized polemical confrontation like fish need water. Just so the reader knows where I am coming from – it is only fair – I tend to fall among the modernizers myself, though on occasion I find myself in agreement with the eternal romantics. I do not think I really fit the profile of the country collector, though I must concede that sometimes they seem to be the ones who appear to have the best time traveling, and that is also a lesson to be learned.

Just as I was done with all this thinking, we landed at Bangkok international airport. A pretty impressive structure, and yet one that is going to be superseded by a brand new terminal being constructed as I landed. It is said it will impress the world. I am sure it will, Thailand can do it.

2. HELLO INDOCHINA

Bangkok is far and away the biggest hub for all South East Asia travel. My travel mates were coming in on a Royal Jordanian flight from Rome via Amman, and we planned to meet at Bangkok airport and connect together on Bangkok Air to Cambodia. We met at an air-conditioned lounge, small but very bright and pretty. There was a counter with hyper-cold water, tropical juices and fresh fruits available as well as two high-speed internet stations at our disposal, pretty impressive by any standards.

Bangkok Air is rightly famous for pampering its passengers, this would a be First Class only treat in Europe. The several photographers amongst us got together in a corner and compared our arsenals of cameras and lenses, loaded film, checked batteries, and spent time making fun of each other's equipment (it looked like clouds were gathering for a Nikon vs Canon challenge-round over the next several weeks). After a couple of hours we were on our way.

Ravioli and ricotta, the mushy meal served on the sleek Bangkok Air turboprop that delivered us to the land of the Khmer would be the last fleeting flash of Europe for a long time and its totally un-Italian taste was a potent reminder we were now in a truly foreign land.

The sky darkened quickly in the late afternoon and by the time we entered Cambodian airspace it was pitch black; no luck with the first "sunset over the jungle" pictures I had planned to take.

A tropical summer night welcomed us at the airport of Siem Reap (pronounced *Seem Reep*), the modern city which rises next to the ruins of ancient Angkor – which means "the Capital" in Khmer, and was indeed the capital of the Khmer Empire from the 9th century to 1431, when the Emperors moved to Phnom Penh's region. The air was hot, very hot, completely still, and invasively sticky under my shirt. Pearls of sweat began to form on my forearms as I descended the plane's ladder, before I had even had a chance to touch the Cambodian soil.

The few uncertain floodlights which punctuated our solitary airplane's parking area cast an eerie spell over the tarmac. After a short walk, we were directed into the arrivals building. At passport control, two lines formed under a battery of lazy fans which churned the air from the ceiling above: first we lined up to have our passports checked, then again to get a visa. Funny, usually you get a visa first and then have your passport checked and stamped, but never mind.

Filling out the colorful Cambodian customs forms which the stewardess handed out was easy: none of us had any of the items listed as "PROHIBITED GOODS" like arms, ammunition, drugs or …wireless transmitters and receivers! I guessed this meant walkie-talkies, but since access to information was quite tightly controlled in Cambodia perhaps it referred to radio receivers. Pheeeewwww, was I lucky to have forgotten my loyal little short-wave radio which I always carry with me when I travel abroad to listen to the BBC World Service or Radio France International. After years of carrying it around in authoritarian countries in Eastern Europe and Africa I would have hated to see it confiscated by the Cambodian customs.

Even better, none of us had walkie-talkies, I suppose it could have been a threat to Cambodian national security if we had started chatting over the air waves while on a jungle trek, or perhaps the authorities feared that these devious instruments of uncontrollable communication would end up in the hands of guerrillas who could threaten the established order. In fact I was sure that guerrillas who were still active in the Cambodian jungle had no problem getting a hold of walkie-talkies.

At the end of the visa line we had the first direct experience of the petty corruption for which some South East Asian border posts are deservedly notorious. We all needed a Cambodian visa, right now, but would later require a Laotian visa in the continuation of our travels. We had been made aware that Laotian visa offices had a peculiar habit of refusing a visa unless they could slap it on a perfectly virgin page of a visitor's passport.

Loredano had only one blank page left in his well worn passport, and therefore he requested to have his full page sized Cambodian visa – for which each of us had to pay twenty US dollars, several days' wages for an average Cambodian – placed on top of an old and faded Italian stamp, which sat alone and forgotten on another, otherwise virgin clean, page. This way, he would be able to use the blank page for the Laotians a few days later. Knowing the guys in uniform on the other side of the table could be difficult, he pragmatically offered a little tip of two dollars for this special favor.

I obviously was, and remain, opposed to bribing one's way to get what one has a right to, especially if that right has just been purchased with twenty dollars. However, when small sums of money are involved, it sometime pays to be practical and a little tip can save hours of aggravation. It is not right, but it is not worth wasting one's time on. "No problem", said the officer in charge of visas, keeping his cool but obviously smelling blood in broken but unequivocal English, "but that will be ten dollars". What? Loredano looked at me in disbelief as his jaw dropped.

Ten dollars just to put a visa sticker on one page of a foreign passport instead of another page? Roberto urged Loredano to pay up and shut up, it was late in the day, we were tired and we might have had problems with the Laotian consulate later. Outraged, Loredano refused to pay a ten dollar bribe after hardly ten minutes in the country and his bright green Cambodian visa landed, implacably, on his passport's only blank page. And the Laotian visa? We would cross that bridge when we got there, though we feared the ten dollars saved today from the greedy Cambodian officer might end up costing even more when we would have to face his Laotian colleagues.

With that awkward start, we were out of the airport.

On the way to the improbably named *Freedom Hotel* – as of 2002, there was still precious little freedom in Cambodia except on paper documents such as the Constitution and on hotel signs – we passed by a row of spotless new or renovated hotels which have sprouted up after the country opened to international tourism in the early nineties. They mostly catered to the hordes of foreign visitors who fly in and out of Siem Reap in organized package tours to spend a couple of days in the magnificent ruins of Angkor. These hotels appeared as magnificent oases of impeccable comfort, all the more in stark contrast with their surroundings of dark muddy roads, precarious shacks of corrugated sheet and dusty street markets. They glittered with tastefully arranged halogen lights which illuminated individual palm trees, walkways and fountains.

For anything between two hundred and two thousand US dollars a night one could be completely insulated from the reality of life in Cambodia. Once inside one of these resorts, you could be forgiven for thinking you were in Bali, or on a Thai island. To each his own.

We and they

As we drove by the luxury lane to our hotel, I wondered, what was the point of visiting a country as poor as Cambodia – per capita gross national product just a bit over one thousand US dollars per year – and spending most of one's time in these artificial capsules of otherworldly luxury? Why go to Cambodia to sleep how no ordinary Cambodian would ever sleep, where a night in a superior suite cost easily more than a year's average salary? To eat food which was probably quite good but bore little resemblance to the average fare of Cambodians? To be driven to and from the sights in softly cushioned air-conditioned buses? Surely, to get a better idea of this country, like of any country, one should try to get closer to the ways the people live, eat, work, play, and move around as they do, should one not?

I confess I felt a sort of superiority complex as our little rattling van headed toward the dimly lit *Freedom Hotel*, where real Cambodians come to stay and eat together with budget tourists from all over the world. I also felt some contempt for those arrogant western or Japanese tourists who traveled to visit the world but always expected to find the same infrastructure they have at home and were easily disappointed when they did not.

And yet, as I kept thinking about it (the road past the fancy hotels had become muddy and potholed, and it was slowing us down) it appeared to me that this question was not so simple. Yes, staying at these fenced off artificial oases precluded these visitors (mostly country collectors and modernizers, but sometimes, inconsistently, eternal romantics) a more direct contact with Cambodia, but that, in the end, was their problem, and no one else's.

And what was the alternative? How much more of a direct experience were we really going to get just because we would be closer to a few more Cambodians, with whom however we would have precious little substantial interaction? As far as the Cambodians themselves were concerned, these hotels provided jobs, far more jobs than the twenty-dollars-a-day *Freedom Hotel*. They attracted high-income tourists who would otherwise not visit the country at all; moreover, they would not just spend for their hotel but would eat out in premium restaurants, buy the most pricey souvenirs, etc. that is to say they would inject loads of money into the local economy. Even if the big international investors who owned most of these hotels repatriated some of the profits, the posh tourists would provide jobs for far more Cambodian families than we budget travelers.

We, on the other hand, would spend very little, and provide only a very marginal economic contribution.

Only the most obstinate eternal romantic would argue that injecting more money into the local economy and providing more jobs is a bad thing. Funnily enough, such people, whom I would describe as the ultimate conservatives, in the sense that they strive to save the old ways, no matter what, are usually found on the left of the political spectrum. They would probably reject to be so labeled, except perhaps they would see themselves as conservatives inasmuch as the environment in concerned. Not conservatives, conservationists, but the etymology of the two words is the same, it means you resisted change.

Not to speak of the fact that the western and Japanese (now even Russian and Chinese) who checked in at the grand hotels would spend a far more comfortable holiday than we would at the Freedom, and what was wrong with that? We all lived at home in ways which an average Cambodian would not dream of, what is the point in pretending to be like them for a few weeks, dipping our toes through the surface of the pond of underdevelopment (or poverty, or traditional ways or whatever one wants to call it) and then retreating back to our consumerism? Who were we trying to fool?

Not the Cambodians, they were quite aware of the material gap between us and them, and far the most part they wanted to bridge it. Maybe, in the end, we were trying to fool ourselves. When visiting an exotic country, we loved to feel genuinely local for a few weeks and came out persuaded this was a more real, genuine experience than if we had admitted all along that we are not, will never be and do not want to be like the locals. We were only visiting, as tourists, business travelers, aid workers, peacekeepers, whatever, and we were not like the Cambodians, not by any stretch of the imagination, not even close, not even for a single minute.

The hands that see

In about thirty minutes we had covered the distance from the airport to the *Freedom Hotel*. We had hardly checked in when we noticed a small sign behind the counter which advertised massage by the *Seeing Hands*. Custom had it that many massage parlors are a prerogative of the blind in Cambodia; there were dedicated training centers to give these unfortunate fellows who did not see with their eyes a chance to see with their hands and make a decent living.

These were serious massage enterprises, no *sexcapades* envisaged. I was sure one could get a "special" massage, with a "happy ending" in Siem Reap if one wanted to, but we did not look for them and they were never surreptitiously offered to us. Or perhaps they were but we just did not get it, who knows, we were tired... We dropped our luggage off in our rooms and five of us booked a one-hour session of massage. It was advertised as a "Thai Massage", which contrary to some popular beliefs is a very chaste experience. There is no use of any oils or creams and no skin contact: we would change into a white cotton robe covering the whole body.

After a short van ride, we were in a dark side street in downtown Siem Reap. In no time we were lying down on five beds in an otherwise empty room which looked a bit like a hospital ward and was equipped with neon lights, a couple of cranky fans and a Japanese air conditioning unit. Most importantly, the window shutters all had mosquito nets, not an insignificant detail since this was the rainy season malaria was pretty much endemic, though not so severe in towns as in the jungle. The air-con unit was the reason why our massage cost six dollars an hour, it would have been three dollars in a non air-con room but it was so hot and it was our first day so we decided to splurge.

Yet, as I changed into the white robe which I found on my bed, it was a bit disturbing to reckon that one hour of operation of a Japanese air-con unit was priced at fifteen dollars (three dollars surcharge times five of us sharing its use), ie the same price of one hour of work of four trained Cambodian masseuses and one masseur. But then I thought that if this was what the (mostly foreign) clients wanted, why not?

At three dollars per hour per person over and above the price of the massage itself, the association of the *Seeing Hands* must have paid off the Japanese machine fairly quickly and then make a handsome profit. We were told the money was used to help the blind, there were no third parties involved. As I handed them the cash I hoped this was indeed the case, I did not feel so bad anymore after all and got ready to enjoy the treat.

Odd, after twenty-four hours of intercontinental travel we landed at night in the middle of a completely foreign country and the first people with whom we had any significant human interaction were a team of young blind masseurs and masseuses. As they found their way a bit awkwardly around the room, and then, confidently, around our shrouded bodies, we could not help first cautiously smiling and then laughing at the scene... and at each other, as some – I, for one – were a bit ticklish at the soft touch of the Seeing Hands deploying onto our bodies! For a moment, I feared we might be perceived as disrespectful; as they could not see us perhaps they might have thought we were laughing at them. But there we were, lying flat in our clean white robes and enjoying the careful but very firm and sure touch of the Seeing Hands.

Then, the five of them immediately broke out in a loud irrepressible giggle of their own that would continue, on and off, interspersed with only a few spoken words, until an hour later, when we left the premises... Were they laughing at us? Well, surely not at the way we looked in our silly white robes – last time I had seen myself in one was at some toga party at Georgetown a quarter of a century earlier – since they cannot see us! Was our language funny? Was our own laughter contagious?

They must have heard this kind of reaction from first timers so many times, and clearly they did not understand a word of what we are saying. It was actually the four masseuses who were doing most of the laughing, the masseur perhaps did not feel too well, as he kept coughing; to be polite, while massaging Luca, he would turn his head when coughing and direct his virally charged exhalation toward the intake of the air-conditioning unit, which of course would immediately spit it out nice and cold for all the rest of us in the room to breathe. No matter, they just kept laughing. Perhaps they were just exchanging the latest town gossip, how presumptuous of me it was to think they had to be speaking about us.

After all, our relationship with them was absolutely asymmetrical. Everything about them was new to us: it was our first day in their country, the first such interaction with a group of blind people, most of the environment was also new. But to them, we must have been just another five bodies, more or less the same type of foreign, unintelligible bodies, under the same white robes, as they must have gotten pretty much everyday, several times a day.

Anyway, considering they were working late in the evening, they seemed to be having a jolly good time, and we did too... a good way to start a journey in Cambodia. We paid our six dollars each to a staff member who could see very well, carefully counted the greenbacks and thanked us with a big smile. And after a few minutes we were blissfully fast asleep back at the *Freedom Hotel*.

2. Angkor Wat bas-relief

3. TEMPLES AND TETRAMELES: MAJESTIC RUINS AND TRAGIC HISTORY

The mid-afternoon squall hit with but a few minutes' warning. I was in the middle of a large courtyard at Ta Prom, the largest of the temples of Angkor, negotiating my way amidst ancient crumbling stone walls and overgrown roots. Ta Prom is the second most famous of the *wat* (temples) of Angkor, the largest and the most picturesque, if not as famous as the Angkor Wat. The reason for its unique charm is that, during successive waves of restorative work, it was decided to leave most of it much the way it was when it was found, after four centuries of abandon, in the mid-XIX century. Tropical vegetation still covers most of it, especially huge spung trees (aka *tetrameles*) whose roots enveloped the immense stone building blocks like the tentacles of a giant octopus.

The crashing monsoon rain was thick, determined, unforgiving and noisy, almost to the point of being overwhelming. The water level on the ground immediately began to rise (the ancient Khmer draining system either was wanting or, more likely, was clogged up, as the modern Khmer had not done anything about it yet) and after a half hour or so the awesome courtyard was transformed into a murky pond. Local guides waded across, ankle-deep in the brown water, looking for their clients who had sought shelter in those structures which still stand in defiance of centuries of assault from both nature and man.

As the rain poured from above my roofless temple tower I stood with a few others under the entrance vault; the walls were so thick that even without a roof I could keep dry if I was careful to keep my balance on the threshold. Inside the tower, a weird echo transformed our multilingual chatter in a true Babel.

The rain was a nuisance but the atmosphere it created was magic. For one, as the hordes of tourists disappeared from the open areas trying to keep dry inside the temples, it was finally possible to admire the unobstructed view of the awesome structures. The sight of the stark silhouettes of dark stone were veiled by a glittering curtain of massive amounts of rainwater. The rumbling rainfall, the dark sky, the unrelenting heat and the austere ruins suddenly emptied of people contributed to create a mystical ambience: it all looked unreal, it felt as if we were in a film studio, and I looked around to see if Indiana Jones was about to make a sudden appearance…

As I waited, standing powerless for the rain to stop, I could not escape thinking about the past of Angkor. This great civilization was falling from its peak while in Europe the Renaissance was in full bloom, but there were no important contacts between the two. Marco Polo did not come here. It was then abandoned in 1431, when the Khmer kings moved the capital to Phnom Penh.

Since then it had only occasionally been visited by European traders, none of whom wrote much about it. I then zoomed fast forward a few centuries. While the heavy stones themselves have largely withstood the test of time, some of the architecture did not. When Henri Mouhot arrived at Angkor in 1860, the structures had been almost entirely swallowed by the jungle, as one can still see in a few places, like here at Ta Prom, where the invasion of nature has been left untouched for effect.

Moving forward still in history, and coming disturbingly close to our days, I tried to imagine the desperate plight of the thousands who sought refuge here in 1975. When the Khmer Rouge took power in April of that year, their first initiative was to order the evacuation of all Cambodian cities. This was an essential first step to implement their mad plan for a pure agrarian and autarchic society. In a matter of days, they displaced the nation's entire urban population, scattering it about the countryside. To avoid resistance, people were told they would only be away from home for a few days, and that therefore they did not need to carry anything with them – that also ensured a richer booty was available when Khmer Rouge gangs on the loose looted the empty cities.

We would be here another couple of hours, maybe a little longer, and while I was uncomfortable with the rain and heat, my most serious problem was really just protecting camera and lenses from flooding. Come evening time, a warm dinner and an air conditioned room, even at the cheap *Freedom Hotel*, would ease my sleep in a clean bed.

They, on the contrary, were hiding here to escape deportation to forced labor camps and the killing fields. They were pursued by ruthless adolescent soldiers who killed at whim and, to prevent city dwellers from hiding or running away from where they were ordered to go, terrorized them by wantonly planting millions of land mines all over the place, in rice fields, around monuments – many of which are unaccounted for and still buried around the countryside, occasionally emerging from the mud to kill and maim people, many of whom were not even born when the Khmer Rouge were in power.

Those wretched refugees experienced the same monsoon squalls I was seeing today, but had no hot food, let alone a bed, to look forward to, only the stone floors of the ruins to lie on and swarms of mosquitoes for company. They did not know for how long they would be able to evade the advancing Khmer Rouge fanatics – hours, days, weeks? – and were suddenly forced on the run, time and again, with families often becoming separated for good and the weak and the old dying on the way. It was beyond me to try to imagine such untold horror unfolding amidst these timeless, majestic monuments of the great Khmer civilization.

That was not the last violence the monuments had to endure. After the Vietnamese overthrew the Khmer Rouge in Phnom Penh, battles continued in this part of the country for years, and in the 1980s Khmer Rouge and Vietnamese forces joined door to door battles at Angkor, thus causing even more senseless damage to the structures. Bas-reliefs which had survived for centuries, enduring the onslaught of yearly monsoons and the enveloping action of giant tropical vegetation, were blown to smithereens in a matter of days by the cross fire of opposing Communist armies.

A second day at the ruins of Angkor and I began to feel more comfortable in the company of the Khmer gods. Heat and humidity were merciless, but I was getting used to them.

The hike up the Kbal Spean hill was pleasant despite the heat. An uneven path cut through the jungle, leading up to the "one thousand lingams". The *lingam,* considered by some to be the representation of the phallus of Shiva, is often considered an Indian symbol of male prowess. Well, there were actually no more than a few hundred of them, and they were not real lingams but symbolic representations of lingams, just little round half-spheres carved into the stone in and along a stream. The stream itself was actually the main reason to be here in the first place, as the vivacious running water makes what might otherwise have turned out to be a dud of a trip a lively and sparkling place. OK this would not be the highlight of my stay in Cambodia, but the combination of ancient art, virgin jungle and running torrent of clear water was worth the effort of the ascent.

On the way down, on a different part of the hill, the river had a pleasant surprise in store: about half way to the bottom of the valley the water dropped off a cliff for about five meters, splashing noisily into a large natural swimming pool. This made it possible to enjoy a most pleasing water massage for the many Cambodians and assorted foreigners who come here for the sole reason of taking this cool invigorating shower. My friends quickly changed and jumped in; I initially hesitated, as vicious images of tropical micro-organisms leaping from the water into my mouth, nose and ears formed in my still antiseptic western mind. I could just imagine these bilharzia larvae whetting their appetite upon seeing all those succulent host bodies get into perfect positions in the water for them to tag on to. I could just about feel them penetrating my skin, working their way through tissue and beginning to feed on my vital organs.

After a few minutes, however, the evil images wither away, killed off by the humidity and heat perhaps; I also thought the chances of bilharzia being released into the water by infected human excretion up the river was small, as there were no settlements upstream. Thus reassured, I joined the others under the waterfall, in a spot where gravity made the water strike my upper body just right, energetically but not violently. It was addictive: once the water began to massage my shoulders and its coolness pervaded my whole person, I was ready to sign up for an all afternoon session.

I left after a few minutes, but I just could not bring myself to wipe my body dry and put my clothes back on; I had to go back under the waterfall. It was as if some sort of unknown and hitherto bottled up secret energy had been released from deep inside my whole body whilst it was under the pressure of water dropping on my neck and biceps, and it gave an intense and persistent pleasure. I then lay down in the company of some lizards on some large smooth boulders to dry body and clothes before resuming the march down to the bottom of the valley.

A short lunch break allowed me to slurp away at a fresh coconut while I sat in the shade and watched the crowds go by. The most interesting part of eating this particular coconut was watching the young waitress prepare it for me. She was incredibly dexterous in handling a very substantial machete. First she would chop off the head and the tail of the coconut. Next, she would use part of the hard shell to make a sort of spoon which we could use to scrape the tender white pulp of the fruit when I was done sipping its juice with a straw. Maybe it was the heat but, even after having exerted my muscles way more than on an average day, a coconut was enough for my lunch. I just needed some sugar and hydration.

With hindsight, it was far more inspiring to admire Angkor a day earlier while getting soaked under that heavy afternoon squall. For the remainder of my time I and my companions would be elbowing our way through throngs of tourists in postcard perfect sunny days. Travelers beware: make sure you visit Angkor during the summer monsoon season, avoid those boring sunny months! Or, alternatively, get up before dawn and sneak inside before the other tourists are done with breakfast!

Suggested Reading: The Way of the Kings

Claude and Perken meet on an ocean liner heading for Indochina, and throw in their lots together to form a dual expedition into the perilous Cambodian jungles of the 'Way of the Kings'. Claude, a young Frenchman, is seeking adventure, fame, and money; Perken, an experienced Dutch explorer, is returning to his own little patch of Siam, aiming to recapture his former masculine pride, and appalled by the coming of age and its effects. The two face death at every turn from the seething forest and 'bestial' tribes people, but are driven to leave their stamp on a world on the eve of its demise, in defiance of the advance of the railroad and 'civilisation', and the term of their own fragile lives.

Novel by André Malraux, a kind of Conradian "Heart of Darkness" set in Cambodia. It is a great introduction to the atmosphere of the temples, at least the way the temples were before mass tourism, and to the jungle. Also an introspective search into our own souls as travelers.

(The Way of the Kings, by André Malraux, English edition by Hesperus Press, 2005.)

3. Nature takes over at Ta Prom

4. SILK AND LAND MINES

T he only reason why most travelers choose to include Siem Reap in their tour of South East Asia is the archeological site of Angkor, recognized by UNESCO as a World Heritage site and without a doubt one of the great artistic and architectural achievements of all time. Many come to Cambodia only for Angkor, flying in and out from Thailand. Without Angkor, few outside Cambodia would ever even know of Siem Reap. Yet, there is far more that deserves attention in this corner of Asia.

The Land Mines Museum

One reason why more people should travel to Siem Reap, and why those who do should perhaps factor in an extra day, is to learn about the work of Mr. Aki Ra. He is the founder and director of the Landmine Museum of Siem Reap. As a student of international security issues, I was familiar with the fact that Cambodia was one of the most heavily mined countries in the world, a record contested only by Afghanistan, Mozambique and Angola. The International Committee for the Ban of land mines, recipient of the Nobel Peace Prize in 1997, estimates that there are over 35,000 amputees injured by land mines in Cambodia.

When we asked to go visit the Landmine Museum our local guide, who usually extolled the wonders of each site we visited in turn, strangely made no comment at all. After a short ride through town, we filed past a row of impeccable modern housing projects for the army (the only spic and span buildings in Siem Reap seem to be the luxury hotels for foreigners, the army housing and the offices of the Cambodian People's Party) and came to a halt in front of an iron gate. A chain was strung across two metal poles; it was held down on either side by defused hand grenades and it blocked the entrance. There were no signs announcing what it was that we were about to enter. An officer sitting at a small table on one side asked us to pay three dollars each to get in, which we did, and once inside we were welcomed by an old Soviet helicopter and a wrecked MiG fighter aircraft standing forlorn in a yard.

At this point I began to be suspicious: we were obviously on military premises but the Landmine Museum was described in our guidebook as a non governmental organization, and this was not it. A quick look around and we realized we were in a military museum, which included, inter alia, a copious display of land mines, but we are not at THE Landmine Museum. The disappointment was compounded by the realization we had just contributed our entrance fee dollars not to a worthy charity but to the army budget, or, worse, to who knows which officer's pockets!

The Army Museum was an open air graveyard of rusty weapons and gruesome pictures from the war, not completely uninteresting as such, but rather dull and uninformative. Heavy weapons systems (tanks, artillery) were thrown around the gardens at random. A few open shelves displayed defused grenades, anti-tank mines, Kalashnikovs, heavy machine guns and a number of other assorted light weapons. All of them were simply laid out for everyone to see, touch and easily steal.

There were no guards looking over the displays. It would have been quite easy to grab some of the smaller guns, put it in a hand bag and walk away. If this was any indication of the care with which authorities practice gun control, it was no wonder that so many guns got into the wrong hands in Cambodia, to the point that "No Guns Allowed" signs are routinely seen in public areas, right next to more familiar "No Smoking" ones. Anyway I did not steal anything, but was happy to ask Roberto to take some photos of myself wearing a helmet and manning a thoroughly rusted and ammunition-less heavy machine gun that was lying on the ground next to an even more rusted helicopter.

As we left the Army Museum in a fairly somber mood, I had a hard time trying to persuade the others to go to yet another war sight. Time for shopping, cried impatiently the majority of my travel companions! After a quick tour of a handicraft shop it was almost dark, but happily we were on our way to the real Landmine Museum. Our van struggled on the heavily potholed road (with a somewhat morbid grin, I could not help to wonder whether they tested their land mines here or what?) that took us through some of the humble suburbs of Siem Reap, filled with roaming farm animals of all shapes and sizes, an interesting sight in itself. We were tired at the end of a long day and I feared the wrath of my travel companions if for some reason this did not work out to be as interesting as I had made it to be...

When our guide told us we had arrived it really did not look like we were at a museum at all. Across a brittle iron gate we found ourselves in the small garden of what looked like one of the many flimsy suburban dwellings of Siem Reap we had driven by to get there. That must have been what it was, at least originally. A couple of dozen saplings were planted in the ground, with anti-tank land mines at their side. A small table displayed printed landmine awareness T-shirts and hats. A few fliers in different languages told the story of Mr. Aki Ra, a former Khmer Rouge conscripted child soldier who worked as a mine-clearing specialist and museum curator, who had to overcome many problems to carry on with his work.

He was born around 1970 (he was not sure) and became an orphan when his parents were taken away by the Khmer Rouge. He later served in the army and laid many mines on the Thai border himself. Later he joined a United Nations campaign to rid the country of the threat of leftover ordnance. Eventually he founded this museum in 1997. In it I could see faded black and white photos of the war, some military paraphernalia and thousands of bombs and mines of all shapes and sizes, but above all the small but deadly anti-personnel mines that were the country's enduring reminder of the civil conflict. And also the larger, pizza-shaped mines designed to blow up tanks or armored vehicles. You could even buy some empty shells, and I was tempted, but it was heavy stuff to carry around over the next few weeks while I travel, and I was not sure it would make it through security controls at the various airports I would have to go through before reaching home.

There was no entrance fee, but a donation of 3 dollars was suggested, which we all happily handed over. I bought a square red "DANGER MINES!" sign, made of cardboard, thousands of which we could still see all over the Cambodian countryside to warn people off fields which have not been cleared yet. I also bought a grey T-shirt with the museum logo and the same square red "DANGER MINES!" sign.

4. The author at the Army Museum, Siem Reap

5. Unusual souvenir: a common road sign in Cambodia

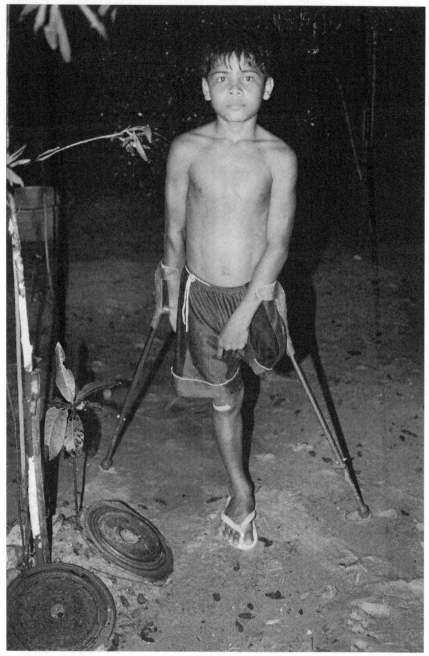

6. Victim of land mines (visible at bottom left)

Silk bites

The following day, my mind still overflowing with images of land mines and mutilated youth, could not have started with a starker contrast: a visit to a silk farm. The venue was peaceful, silent, as the smooth tissue was produced and prepared for the market.

We visited the mulberry field where the food for the worms is grown, and a guide explained all the various stages of production. Always interesting, even though I knew the process already, and every time I cannot help but feel sorry for the worms who are boiled alive in their cocoons to extract the silk thread.

But the novelty, most interesting for me, was when they explained that, once the cocoon is removed, the worms are not thrown away, but... eaten! I must have looked very skeptical because the guide said that if I did not believe him I could see for myself, or even better try a bite or two! Never shy for new experiences, I said I would indeed be interested.

He led me to a corner where the boiled white worms, thoroughly cleaned, or so I hoped, were piled up in a bowl for processing. He invited me to taste one, which I did with some circumspection. The thick white worm I picked amongst many looked clean and did not have any smell. I put it on my tongue and it did not have much of a taste either, it felt more like a piece of overcooked squid. It was definitely the strangest food in my life, so far.

He assured me it was very nutritious. I supposed that, despite the high-temperature boiling, the flesh would deliver a reasonable amount of proteins, but it could definitely use some sauce to become more palatable. I would later search for dishes of silkworms in many restaurants we visited, but to no avail. Anyway, the fact that the worms are eaten made me feel better, their lives had acquired a second purpose, to feed people in addition to providing expensive cloth.

The miniatures of Dy Proeung

Another reason to spend a bit more time in Siem Reap than is necessary to see Angkor is to visit Dy Proeung. He was born sometime in 1936, and was an artist and an trained architect. He had long been involved in the preservation of his country's heritage.

His current multi-year project was the chiseling of a miniature Angkor Wat, Bateay Srei and other temples in his garden museum. He made his own molds and used cement to shape the scale model buildings. His first project however was a detailed mapping of Angkor, and he labored at it for many years with some colleagues in the 1960s. The result was a large book, of which few copies were printed. He had one single copy for himself.

He was 39 years old when the Khmer Rouge came looking for the book of blueprints of the temples in the 1970s. They had heard of this work, which they considered reactionary, and wanted to destroy everything that belonged to the "old" Kampuchea, to make room for the new society that was brewing in their delirious minds. The year 1975, when they took power, was dubbed *Year Zero*, meaning the beginning of a whole new era. He knew that if his drawings had been found he would be classified as an intellectual and killed. So he buried his book under a thin layer of dirt, away from his dwelling.

He was arrested nonetheless, when working the fields away from town, because someone working with him had stolen food. They were often hungry, but stealing food was usually punished with summary execution. He was saved only because his brother was a doctor working for the communists. After the fall of the regime he recovered the drawings and now he planned to spend the rest of his life to preserve them and disseminate the knowledge of ancient Khmer architecture.

His work gained him some fame, so that he is proud to say he was visited by King Sihanouk. (Yes, since 1993 Cambodia is once again a monarchy, though the king is no more than a figurehead. Uniquely, I think, to Cambodia, the king is elected by a nine-member Royal Council, and the title is not automatically inherited by the incumbent's offspring.)

Long live Dy Proeung, and any visitor to Siem Reap should visit and pay tribute to this remarkable man and his creations.

Chicken, fish and coconuts

Dinner tonight was special, we found a small restaurant that offered *amok* fish, a Cambodian specialty. The fish was cleaned of bones and chopped up in bite-sized chunks, Chinese style, then marinated and steamed in a sort of Indian style curry based on coconut milk. Some herbs provide the enticing aroma that pervaded the room and whetted my appetite. I could figure out lemongrass was in there, but could not be sure about the others. The fish fillets are then steamed in banana leaves, that later double as plates, and this tends to firm up the consistency of the dish. White rice on the side provided the necessary carbs.

The amok fish was excellent but the portions not too generous and I was hungry after a long day of walking, so I ordered some amok chicken, which was served to me in the hard shell of a coconut. I am not sure this qualified as an iconic Cambodian dish in the same way as the amok fish, but its sweet tendency was no less appealing.

Cambodian cuisine, like most aspects of the national culture, clearly shows why Indochina is called Indochina: the influence of the two big cousins, India and China, is unmistakable. And the result is a delicate and unique balance of flavors and aromas, ranging from spicy to sweet-and-sour.

I asked to visit the kitchen of this eatery and the owner was happy to oblige. A small room, with large gas bottles powering fire under a few pots. The blackened walls betrayed a well-oiled (literally and figuratively) enterprise, and the smiling ladies who welcomed my appearance were clearly amused when I started taking photographs. They cracked up laughing when I asked them to pose for me!

Oh, I could not find out what the word "amok" meant in this context. If you look it up in a dictionary, "running amok" means the sudden and violent surge of a mob in desperate attack, it is one of the few words from traditional South East Asian languages that made it into the international vocabulary. How that applied to fish and chicken remains a mystery to me.

The evening ended with another visit to the *Seeing Hands* massage parlor. We would miss them when we left, I know that, so I would not pass another opportunity tonight. Or perhaps I was overly worried, they told us there were other similar businesses in other towns in Cambodia. When we got there they welcomed us with a cheerful smile.

This time they even set up a curtain for us to modestly change out of sight. Not their sight, obviously, but our own. Some of the girls made use of it, we boys didn't. I wondered why. The next hour was a blissful mix of soft music and energetic massage applied through our white robes. It was quite hot, but a few vintage fans on the ceiling whirred the stickiness away. I was very sorry to have to get up and return to the hotel.

Suggested reading: Sideshow

William Shawcross interviewed hundreds of people of all nationalities, including cabinet ministers, military men, and civil servants, and extensively researched U.S. Government documents. This full-scale investigation – with material new to this edition – exposes how Kissinger and Nixon treated Cambodia as a sideshow. Although the president and his assistant claimed that a secret bombing campaign in Cambodia was necessary to eliminate North Vietnamese soldiers who were attacking American troops across the border, Shawcross maintains that the bombings not only spread the conflict, but led to the rise of the Khmer Rouge and the subsequent massacre of a third of Cambodia's population.

This is far and away the best book on the Cambodian campaign waged by Nixon during the Vietnam War. It contains meticulous research, a wealth of data and some good insights. The appendix to the book, with Kissinger's rebuttal and the author's reply, are particularly useful.

It would have been even better but for the palpable political bias that transpires throughout the book. The author hates the guts of Nixon and Kissinger, and anything the United States ever did in this book is always inevitably wrong.

This emotional approach detracts from the necessary detachment and cold blood I believe to be indispensable in any historical research work, especially when focussing on topics as controversial as this one.

(Sideshow — Nixon, Kissinger and the Destruction of Cambodia, by William Shawcross, Rowman & Littlefield Publishers, revised edition 2002.)

The "Vietnamese" village

Waking up at the crack of dawn was not so hard as I expected, even after several long days of uninterrupted walking in the jungle and amidst ruins in sweltering heat, aggressive humidity and repeated thunderstorms. Maybe my body clock was still on western European time, so for me it was not early morning but only late evening on the day before.

Or maybe it was the realization that I was about to be swept away for the real, exciting objective of this journey: sailing up the Mekong almost all the way to the Chinese border. The Mekong is a long river, at over 4,900 kilometers it is the tenth longest in the world and the sixth longest in Asia. It starts in Tibet, and flows through southern China, Laos, Cambodia and finally Vietnam, where its imposing delta flows into the South China Sea.

Our van took us out of town, toward the shores of the Tonle Sap Lake, a wide appendix of the Mekong which extends from Siem Reap, at the mouth of the city's eponymous river, almost all the way to the capital. Here is the base of the ferry boat service to Phnom Penh. The night was just fading away, but the air was already warm. All around us, and everything on us, was already damp.

By now I was getting used to being wet (be it because of rain or sweat) as the normal state of being; for the first time in my life I learnt not to even bother to wipe my face, arms or hands, I was just wet and clothes just stuck to my skin, all the time, full stop. I did not mind. Actually, when a breeze would bless me with its delicate caresses, it would cool the sweat on my body and gift a pleasant sensation of coolness. I guess the flip side was that I must have smelled like sweat a lot, but frankly, in this context, I did not care.

The ride to the harbor took about thirty minutes. Along the route, the morning market hawkers were readying their stands to start their trading day. The rumble of motorcycles roaming about the muddy roads began to fill the air. One last time we drove by the magnificent luxury hotels, which at this time were the cocoon of delicate country collectors sleeping their night beautifully away. Most of them had arrived by plane and would leave after a few days' walk among the ruins; few of them would ever see the filthy harbor we were headed to, let alone take their chances to board the creaky but fast hydrofoils for a ride to Phnom Penh: they would fly there.

Pity. That would certainly be faster, more comfortable and safer, but they would miss a whole dimension of Cambodian life. And yet, it does not shame me to confess that for a brief minute I wished I were in one of them. I caught myself day dreaming I was cool and dry, half asleep under a woolen blanket which I had pulled up to my face to mitigate the excessively cold draft flowing from the air-con unit, and was waiting for my breakfast room service boy to knock at the door. It was at this point that a sudden jolt of the van woke me up, and I was happy to be out in the street, enjoying the real Cambodia and about to start a cruise on the Mekong! The flurry of activity all along the riverside was the quintessential flavor of what life was all about in this region of the world.

The harbor was located by the so-called Vietnamese village, which owes its name to the colony of fishermen from Vietnam who have come to fish in the rich waters of the Tonle Sap for ages, taking advantage of the seasonal tides. Many settled here, married locally, became Cambodians. Many kept to themselves, failed to integrate into Khmer society, and social cleavages got deeper.

Over the decades the Khmer, unsurprisingly, did not always display unrestrained affection for the newcomers. Ethnic conflicts flared up time and again. During the repression of the Khmer Rouge regime, Vietnamese-Cambodians received special attention. After the very brief honeymoon between the Khmer Rouge and the newly reunified communist Vietnam it was open conflict, and in fact it was the violence perpetrated against the local Vietnamese community that provided Hanoi with an excellent pretext to invade Cambodia in 1978. By the time of my visit, the official line which both Vietnamese and Cambodians told the world was that the two countries and the two peoples were all great friends, but the reality was not so idyllic. Reports of continued violence and hostility toward Vietnamese fishermen and their families continued to surface through the cover of official denials.

The Vietnamese village itself consisted of a line of huts precariously built on a narrow sliver of land on either side of the road, mostly on stilts. Behind them, one could peek to the open expanse of murky water of the Tonle Sap. As we arrived, the inhabitants of the village were beginning their day. Some were just waking up, others were cooking or eating breakfast, some women were doing their laundry or fetching water for the house, for drinking or washing, others were shaving or bathing, children were playing. All in the same waters. We slowly made our way around the pot holes and looked at what would be a normal scene in any tropical village, as if it was the stage of a theater. The road was very narrow and there was only one row of small one-room huts on either side of it, mostly without doors. We could not avoid intruding into the most private lives of these people, but they must have been so used to travelers on their way to the fast boat filing past every morning that they seemed totally oblivious to our presence.

After perhaps two kilometers of this, we reached a point where the huts ended and a market area began. Here we could witness scenes so common to harbor towns around the developing world. Merchants peddling their wares, fishermen cleaning their catch, young girls approaching boat passengers with cold water bottles. Little boys were diving playfully in the water. There were very few foreigners, almost all passengers getting ready to board the pier were Cambodians carrying heavy loads, maybe to sell in the capital.

Two men carrying a long and thick block of solid ice rushed by. It must have weighed several hundred kilos but each nonchalantly held one end on his bare shoulders while they negotiated their way in the crowd; eventually they delivered it to the fishermen, who broke it up with a sledgehammer and used it to pack their fresh (some still alive) fish for transport to the city markets.

On one side of the market, the fast boats were rather loosely moored to a very basic wooden structure erected on the muddy bank. Our boat was an old long and narrow vessel which looked like a hydrofoil though even when running at full speed it did not really lift itself out of the water as one would have expected. The interior looked like that of an aircraft, with about thirty-five rows of five seats each, two on the right and three on the left of a single narrow aisle. The small round windows too closely resemble, and were as tightly sealed as, those of an airplane. There was but one entrance at the bow. Above the cabin there was a large storage area for luggage, but most of the deck was free for passengers who wanted to enjoy the landscape and the breeze. I took a position comfortably about midship and enjoy watching people getting ready for the trip and started to take pictures as the sun began to rise decisively above the horizon.

A few minutes after seven the boat was gently pushed back from the pier and we were off. At first we proceeded slowly among the last few houses of the Vietnamese village and the myriad small fishing vessels which crowd around the market; all the same, our bow wave rocked rather wildly some of the smaller boats which happen to be closer, but everyone seemed to be used to this treatment and oblivious to the daily routine. As we moved out of the village and onto the wide open Tonle Sap the land widens, boats and stilts gave way to grass, then it was water all around and the hydrofoil convincingly picked up speed. The Mekong was of a deep red ochre, but at times the thick cloud cover reflected on the surface created an enormous somber gray blanket which extended around us in all directions as far as the eye can see.

When the boat reached cruising speed the bow spray began to pound on the upper deck, and the wind-chill froze the fresh water on my body: all of a sudden, for the first time since we arrived in Cambodia, it was not hot and sticky any more, it was actually unbearably cold! As I had no rain gear, it became clear that I could not both go through five hours of this and keep pneumonia at bay. Defying fate, I put my rucksack on, climbed down from the upper-deck and walked along the exposed companionway while holding precariously on a hand rail to try to find protection below deck. I did manage to get inside the cabin and depose myself rather clumsily on an empty seat, and for a moment I thought I was safe. Wrong again!

The air conditioning unit was spewing freezing torrents of air at full blast. As no window could be opened, the room temperature dropped to polar levels. People were wearing sweaters and wind breakers inside! The water sprays I had absorbed while on the top deck became painfully cold on my body. A couple of TV sets were showing a comical play in which three men try to kick each other's bottoms, on each of which a big pink heart is glued. Most passengers seemed to enjoy it; the Cambodian passengers, that is, because it left the rest of us rather perplexed, but obviously much had been lost in translation, or the Cambodian sense of humor must be quite different from ours.

I could not begin to imagine what this place would have looked like in an emergency, say a fire or a major leak. Evacuation would have been a nightmare, or rather, there would probably have been no evacuation, as the only small open door at the bow would have been out of reach for most passengers and the narrow interior corridor would ensure a desperate stampede.

I convinced myself that statistics were on my side; it was like when I was traveling to the interior of Russia or Ukraine for NATO missions. I flew on rattling god-knows-how-old Antonov turboprops: you would hear of the occasional accident, and it would be dangerous to take this trip many times over, but the chances of something happening on this one and only trip were slim.

I wondered what the person in charge of security designs for the ferry line looked like; that such a person existed was for sure, since he or she carefully placed *No Smoking* and *No Guns Allowed* signs on the toilet door. But of course it would be unfair to expect western safety standards in Cambodia, not just yet. Anyway, as no alternatives were available, I retired in fetal position on my seat, turning as far as possible away from the air conditioning vents, wrote a few notes on my diary, hoped for the best and, like many others all around me, dozed off.

After a grand total of five of hours on board, the boat slowed down as the wide Tonle Sap narrows again into the Mekong river and we approached Phnom Penh, where the river banks come much closer together. The noon sun had taken a firm position on top of the sky. There was no more bow spray and it was again dry and hot on the upper deck.

5. THE GHOSTS OF PHNOM PENH

O n our first afternoon in town, soon after we had left our stuff at the hotel, we were hungry and stumbled upon *Antony,* a pizza joint with a presentable collection of French wines to boot. I am always skeptical about Italian food abroad, as it almost invariably adapted to please the taste of local patrons rather than to uphold the sacred culinary tradition of *il bel paese.* My skepticism is reinforced like concrete in places like this, since there were no Italians in sight, so whoever "Antony" was, he could feel free to do whatever he wanted without fear of a raising eyebrows. But there is not too much that can go wrong with pizza after all and this was the only open eatery we could find, so we went in.

Pizza and the soul of Indochina

The only problem was, in the middle of the afternoon, there was no one to make the pizzas. We were served our drinks and some cold foods and the owner said he would go look for the *pizzettaro,* the pizza maker. Which he did, and after a pretty longish wait – but we could not complain, it was the middle of the afternoon, in Italy one would simply have been told to come back in the evening – the pizzas started to make their way to the table, one by one, slightly undercooked but edible.

During the wait, and while munching on my *pizza margherita,* I wondered whether "eternal romantics" would protest about the pernicious globalizing effects of pizza, which preceded McDonalds by many decades as the most ubiquitous standardized food the world over. They might say it hurts local traditions by preventing foreign patrons from tasting local foods and might even create a dangerous and expensive addiction among Cambodians. They who would be drawn away from their healthy gastronomic specialties and pushed toward this round piece of doe with tomato sauce and other assorted bits and pieces on top of it.

Come to think of it, a pizza could be a good symbol of globalization, it also has the right shape, it is round just like the earth. If fact it would even please "flat-earthers" conspiracy theorists! And it is intrinsically democratic, when you share it with friends, with each slice you get an identical piece of the crust and a part of the core, they are normally all the same.

I have never heard an Italian complain about pizza being available all over the world. But many are ready to go up in arms if foreign foods make their way to the streets of our cities. Never mind.

Our bellies replenished for the afternoon, we headed out to town and visited the small hill where the statue of Penh is venerated. Here I sat down in the balmy breeze and read up a bit of history on the origins of this city. This is how I understood the true meaning of Indochina.

This is because, as the name easily suggests, India and China are the two cultural sources of the peoples living here. In Phnom Penh, a pagoda called *Wat Phnom* (Temple Hill) encapsulates this spirit: statues of Buddha and Hindu gods Vishnu and Indra stand side by side in peaceful coexistence. And one should not forget that, for the Hindus, Buddha is but the latest reincarnation of Vishnu.

There was a steady stream of visitors, everyone kept very quiet and some had offerings for the deity. I did not offer anything, I had not thought of it, shame on me, lesson for next time, always bring offers to a holy place. I sat on one side in peaceful contemplation, read a bit and absorbed the mystic atmosphere.

This was a serene start of my visit to the capital, but it was not going to continue like this tomorrow. My next stop, after a good night's rest, was far less spiritual.

"Hill of Poisonous Trees" (Tuol Sleng)

I did not expect this to be a day of such intense and contrasting emotions, but here it was. In a few hours I would visit Khmer Rouge torture centers, be brought to tears at mass killing fields, practice at an army shooting range, ride a motorbike recklessly around town, be sensuously massaged at a restaurant table and drink at a local disco.

It is not a normal thing for a capital city to hold a center of torture and an extermination camp cum mass grave at the top of its "must see" list for visitors. Phnom Penh is anything but your "normal" capital city, however. It was, only a quarter century ago, both the scene and the command headquarters of one of the most hard-to-believe genocidal displays of ruthless, mindless, aimless violence in human history.

It was actually a school in the old days, but the Khmer Rouge turned it into a prison and torture center. When the nightmare they inflicted on their country was over, it became a museum. For future remembrance, it had been kept pretty much like it was when the Vietnamese troops came in 1979. I could see torture beds with shackles, various instruments devilishly designed to inflict unspeakable pain, tiny cells for detention of prisoners and chilling translations of prison regulations. It was too much to describe in words, so here are the words used by the Khmer Rouge themselves, which the museum translated into simple English for the benefits of visitors and posted on a wall.

Khmer Rouge Security Regulations at Tuol Sleng Prison

1. You must answer accordingly to my question. Don't turn them away.

2. Don't try to hide the facts by making pretexts this and that, you are strictly prohibited to contest me.

3. Don't be a fool for you are a chap who dare to thwart the revolution.

4. You must immediately answer my questions without wasting time to reflect.

5. Don't tell me either about your immoralities or the essence of the revolution.

6. While getting lashes or electrification you must not cry at all.

7. Do nothing, sit still and wait for my orders. If there is no order, keep quiet. When I ask you to do something, you must do it right away without protesting.

8. Don't make pretext about Kampuchea Krom in order to hide your secret or traitor.

9. If you don't follow all the above rules, you shall get many lashes of electric wire.

10. If you disobey any point of my regulations you shall get either ten lashes or five shocks of electric discharge.

Urban society had to a great measure overcome the horror – two thirds of all Cambodians alive in 2002 were not even born when the

Khmer Rouge were evicted from the capital city in 1979 and pushed to continue their fight in the jungle. That ratio was even higher in Phnom Penh than in the country as a whole, since urban dwellers were a specific target for physical elimination.

The city itself largely healed from the destruction, though those who knew how it was before the communist takeover contend that it never regained its pre-revolutionary charm. The problem was not only the damage caused by the Khmer Rouge but also the mismanagement of subsequent governments.

Suggested reading: Voices from S-21

The horrific torture and execution of hundreds of thousands of Cambodians by Pol Pot's Khmer Rouge during the 1970s is one of the century's major human disasters. David Chandler, a world-renowned historian of Cambodia, examines the Khmer Rouge phenomenon by focusing on one of its key institutions, the secret prison outside Phnom Penh known by the code name "S-21." The facility was an interrogation center where more than 14,000 "enemies" were questioned, tortured, and made to confess to counterrevolutionary crimes. Fewer than a dozen prisoners left S-21 alive.

During the Democratic Kampuchea (DK) era, the existence of S-21 was known only to those inside it and a few high-ranking Khmer Rouge officials. When invading Vietnamese troops discovered the prison in 1979, murdered bodies lay strewn about and instruments of torture were still in place. An extensive archive containing photographs of victims, cadre notebooks, and DK publications was also found. Chandler utilizes evidence from the S-21 archive as well as materials that have surfaced elsewhere in Phnom Penh. He also interviews survivors of S-21 and former workers from the prison.

Documenting the violence and terror that took place within S-21 is only part of Chandler's story. Equally important is his attempt to understand what happened there in terms that might be useful to survivors, historians, and the rest of us. Chandler discusses the "culture of obedience" and its attendant dehumanization, citing parallels between the Khmer Rouge executions and the Moscow "Show Trials" of the 1930s, the Nazi genocide, the Indonesian massacres in 1965-66, and the Argentine military's use of torture in the 1970s, and the recent mass killings in Bosnia and Rwanda. In each of these instances, Chandler shows how turning victims into "others", in a manner that was

THE GHOSTS OF PHNOM PENH

systematically devaluing and racialist, made it easier to mistreat and kill them.

More than a chronicle of Khmer Rouge barbarism, Voices from S-21 is also a judicious examination of the psychological dimensions of state-sponsored terrorism that conditions human beings to commit acts of unspeakable brutality. (from Amazon's book description)

This book is a useful reference for raw data from some of the protagonists. It is not easy or pleasant reading, in fact rather slow at times, but it does constitute a useful addition to the library of anyone researching the Khmer Rouge.

(Voices from S-21, David Chandler, Silkworm Books, 1999.)

Suggested reading: The Gate

In 1971, on a routine outing through the Cambodian countryside, the young French scholar François Bizot was captured by the Khmer Rouge. Accused of being an agent of American imperialism, he was chained and imprisoned. His captor, a sinister character nicknamed Duch, later responsible for tens of thousands of deaths at the Tuol Sleng prison, interviewed him at length; after three months of torturous deliberation, during which his every word was weighed and his life hung in the balance, he was released. No other western prisoner survived.

Four years later, the Khmer Rouge entered Phnom Penh. Bizot had became the official intermediary between the ruthless conqueror and the terrified refugees behind the gate of the French embassy: a ringside seat to one of history's most appalling genocides.

Bizot was incredibly lucky to see what he saw and come out alive, then move on to survive in Phnom Penh for several more years and write a harrowing and unique account of the Khmer Rouge rule. The gate of the French embassy, where many notables of the old regime had found refuge, and through which they will have to walk to their fate in the hands of the communists.

A unique first-hand experience that very few western writers have been able to share so much in detail. He talks to many revolutionary soldiers, and discusses politics as well as the details of day-to-day existence, the next harvest, education. Reading him is almost as good as having been there, without the dangers and the discomfort!

(The Gate, by François Bizot, Vintage new edition, 2004.)

The Killing Fields

A few amputees guarded the entrance to the shrine. Their faces were somber, their expression resigned and their eyes communicated a deep sorrow. They looked like they were in their thirties, which meant they were probably in their twenties, victims of land mines exploded over the many years of "peace", which continue to this day, when the worst of the civil war is over but millions of mines still littered the fields of Cambodia. We paid a small entry fee (or the upkeep of the shrine) and walked through the door of hell.

Inside the fenced grounds, a huge brick and glass stupa (a holy building originally meant to hold a relic, though very few do these days) had been erected in the middle of a field, and thousands of skulls had been piled inside. Clothes which belonged to the victims were displayed on a separate shelf. It was a grim scene, and it only got worse.

A few meters further ahead, some of the large mass graves had been left as they were found, for people to remember: roughly dug holes in the ground, with torn cloth and bones still sticking out of the mud. A few children helped point the most gruesome corners to us, and asked for pens for tips.

In one place a human jaw lay half-buried in the thick wet dirt, to the point where I confess I wondered whether it had been artfully displayed for the visitors; but it did not really matter, hundred of thousands of jaws do lie, and would remain forever undetected, in the mud of Cambodia. A small display and a site map explained in various languages what this was all about.

I was in the *Choeung Ek Genocidal Center,* one of the "Killing Fields" so well depicted in many books and in the unmissable movie – see my suggested reading and film details below.

Some seventeen thousand people are estimated to have been executed here, a huge number by any standard, and yet only a drop in the ocean of the Khmer Rouge's genocide.

As we left the site, I gave a few riel (the Cambodian currency) to a couple of the amputees who counted on alms to get by. One was grateful, but the other was not; he explained with his hands that I gave his buddy more than I gave to him, which was not true, I gave each the same. He had only one leg, but quickly followed me to the van which was waiting in the parking lot. I did not have any more riel, and in any case it seemed to me to be a bit much that the recipients of alms should also set the standard of what is appropriate to give.

A souvenir shop on the edge of the parking area, selling cheap trinkets, was also a bit out of sync with the character of this site. I feared this mass grave, which should be venerated as a historical admonition to humanity, might acquire a sort of commercial dimension which would trivialize it and did not suit it at all.

On the way back, we were all speechless. A stunned silence pervaded our van, where an hour earlier we had all been cracking jokes in the many Italian dialects spoken in my group of companions. One of the distinguishing characteristics by which you can tell a group of Italians is that they tend to speak all at the same time, no matter how many. That no one was so much as uttering a word was in itself a very loud description of our innermost mood after visiting the killing fields.

Suggested reading: Beyond the Killing Fields

This first-ever anthology of the war reporting and commentary of Pulitzer Prize-winning journalist Sydney Schanberg is drawn from more than four decades of reporting at home and abroad for the New York Times, Newsday, the Village Voice, and various magazines. The centerpiece of the collection is his signature work, "The Death and Life of Dith Pran," which appeared in the New York Times Magazine. This became the foundation of Roland Joffe's acclaimed film The Killing Fields (1984), which explored the Khmer Rouge genocide in Cambodia during the late 1970s.

The book on which the famous movie referred to below was taken.
(Beyond the Killing Fields, Sydney Shanberg, Potomac Books, 2010.

Suggested Reading: First They Killed My Father

Until the age of five, Loung Ung lived in Phnom Penh, one of seven children of a high-ranking government official. She was a precocious child who loved the open city markets, fried crickets, chicken fights and being cheeky to her parents.

When Pol Pot's Khmer Rouge army stormed into Phnom Penh in April 1975, Loung's family fled their home and were eventually forced to disperse to survive. Loung was trained as a child soldier while her brothers and sisters were sent to labour camps. The surviving siblings were only finally reunited after the Vietnamese penetrated Cambodia and started to destroy the Khmer Rouge.

Bolstered by the bravery of one brother, the vision of the others and the gentle kindness of her sister, Loung forged on to create for herself a courageous new life.

This is a personal history of the author during the most atrocious years of the Khmer Rouge rule in Cambodia (1975-1979). I found the greatest value in the book to be her first hand experience of countless episodes of cruelty and sheer madness. She tells those stories calmly and without deep political analysis, as if she did not really understand what was going on. Which, of course, to a large extent she did not, as she was just a child! But this, far from being a weakness, is a strength of the book.

Many books have been written on the politics of the Khmer Rouge regime, and many more will be written as more and more evidence becomes available. However this book will never be out of date, because true first hand experience as candidly seen through the eyes of a child will always be relevant, interesting, and shocking!

A weak point in the book is the parts where she admits she does not know what happened and uses her imagination to fill the gap. Maybe she could have left those parts out altogether. However this in no way detracts from the overall instructional value of the book.

In 2017 this book has been rewritten as a screenplay for a Netflix film produced by Angelina Jolie.

(First They Killed My Father – A Daughter of Cambodia Remembers, by Loung Ung, Mainstream Publishing, 2001.)

Suggested film: The Killing Fields

Scripted by Bruce Robinson it is based on the true story of the relationship between Sydney Schanberg (Sam Waterston), a Pulitzer Prize winning New York Times correspondent, and Dith Pran (Haing S. Ngor), the Cambodian aide who remains behind following the evacuation of Cambodian citizens by the US army.

A not-to-be-missed movie about the Cambodian tragedy of the second half of the 1970s.

(The Killing Fields, by Roland Joffe, 1984.)

The shooting range

To go to Cambodia and to speak of war and guns is one and the same thing. The ubiquitous "No Guns Allowed" signs are a constant reminder that until just a few years ago firearms were as common here as in the "Wild West" of America in the XIX century. They were a bit less common at the time of my visit, at least as far as I could tell. We were nonetheless surprised to learn that the army provided anyone with a few dollars to spare the opportunity to experience the kick of playing Rambo for a few minutes and four of us decided to give it a go – the others went shopping. The most excited to go shooting were the girls!

The road to the shooting range passed by the airport, and I recalled reading how this was the scene of some very real shooting only five years ago, during the latest violent *coup d'etat*. It was mid-afternoon and a traffic jams slowed us down. This was one of the few places where I actually liked traffic jams: for one, it meant we were slower in bumping over the million pot-holes and our backs greatly benefited from it; also, jams were an indication of activity, and while conscious of the problems of sound and air pollution, it was encouraging to see Phnom Penh alive and working its way out of poverty.

After a few kilometers we turned right into what was obviously an army base. A few dozen very young soldiers in smart fatigues were practicing on an obstacle course; practicing for what, now that the war is over, I am not sure. But a large army serves a domestic purpose in Cambodia, it allowed its top brass to claim a larger slice of the state budget and increases their prestige and the perks that go with it.

Just past the obstacle course a small building with a wall display of all kinds of guns was waiting for us. A couple of European tourists who had just completed their shooting were on their way out and we were now alone with a couple of Cambodian officers. In broken English they lead us around the display: Russian, American, Vietnamese, Indonesian rifles, machine guns, pistols, carabines, and a whole host of other rifles unknown to me – shame on me, after working at NATO Headquarters for seven years I cannot even recognize guns...

A few meters further down some targets were ready and waiting for their share of lead bullets. We were presented with a menu, much like what you get in a restaurant, with the prices (in US dollars!) of various kinds of ammunition. Bullets were between 50 and 90 US cents each, depending on the type. This was several times their market cost, but hey there is supposed to be market capitalism in Cambodia now right? We bought a few dozen rounds for the for a Soviet-design AK-47s and an American-design M-16s, two symbols of jungle warfare, two guns that shot at each other in many theaters around the world when Cold War enemies would fight by proxy. Last, we put on our ear muffles and off we went.

I was somewhat disappointed that the M-16 was actually a recent Indonesian copy and not an American original; they did have some of the latter as well, but they were old stuff from the seventies and tended to jam, the officer told us. Oh well, never mind. The officer set the guns on "semi-automatic", ie we had to pull the trigger for each bullet, or else our store of ammos would be through in a few seconds! It was with some trepidation that I started to aim; at first, it was somehow not funny to shoot live ammunition, not here in Cambodia, not after having been to the killing fields. Then, after the first few shots, it all began to feel what it was supposed to feel, ie just target practice for fun.

We shot the target and photographed each other in turns, and after twenty minutes we were done. Before returning the guns I saw some purple flowers on a plant and I could not resist picking a few and taking more pictures with flowers in our gun barrels! The young Cambodians laugh...

Well, I thought that was good, that they could now laugh at guns, it was probably one more sign of the passing of an awful era. Upon leaving the range, I did not especially relish the thought that we had just contributed twenty-five dollars to the budget of the Cambodian army – that is if, and it was a big if, those in charge of the shooting range kept proper accounting of their receipts – but the exhilaration of shooting with an AK-47 and an M-16, I admit, prevailed over any lingering sense of guilt.

Anyway, the problems in the Cambodian army were far more serious. It was way too big for either the defense needs of the country or the government's budget. International donors had given aid to provide opportunity for military personnel to find jobs in the civilian sector of the economy. Soldiers had been offered tractors and sewing machines to help them integrate into the economy, but with mixed results. Much remained to be done.

Afternoon out and about town. I needed to buy some essentials, toothpaste and the like. For that I went to a supermarket that was full to the hilt of imported stuff. Food, drinks, everything seemed quite expensive for a local salary. Maybe it was meant for foreigners. I would have much rather gone to a local market but it was late to go look for one. I also decided to invest a grand total of 1 dollar to buy a water-proof poncho, it would surely be useful in the near future.

A ride in one of the ubiquitous motorcycle-taxis took me to the so-called Russian market. The ride was rather scary, my driver was worse (or better, depending on how you looked at it) than anything I had ever seen in Rome, my city, which is famous (or notorious, depending on how you looked at it) for reckless driving. Of course I had no helmet, and neither did my driver. He zig-zagged around the slow traffic and had no qualms jerking the bike to change lanes and overtaking on the left or on the right, no matter what. To his partial justification I have to say that this is how every other bike rider in sight drove, he was just playing by the rules. I did feel I had put my life on the line at the time, but I must admit that it was fun! I gave him a tip.

At the market itself there is only some mediocre art creations, cheap cloth and lots of material for construction and home decoration. The raw food market was more interesting to photograph but we are not going to do any cooking! Lots of business happening though, it was a sign of a lively economy in the capital city. Who knows why it was called "Russian". Someone suggested because the Russians were the only foreigners to come here during the Soviet times, which may be true, perhaps they were looking for stuff they could not find at home.

Suggested Reading: Off the Rails in Phnom Penh.

Phnom Penh in the 1990s is a city of beauty and degradation, tranquillity and violence, and tradition and transformation; a city of temples and brothels, music and gunfire, and festivals and coups...

But for many, it is simply an anarchic celebration of insanity and indulgence. Whether it is the $2 wooden shack brothels, the marijuana-pizza restaurants, the AK-47 fireworks displays, or the intricate brutality of Cambodian politics, Phnom Penh never ceases to amaze and amuse. For an individual coming from a modern western society, it is a place where the immoral becomes acceptable and the insane becomes normal as they search for love in the brothels or adventure into the dark heart of guns, girls and ganja.

This is an easy book to read. You will earn a genuine view of how debauchery and flimsiness governed this place in the 1990s, at least from the point of view of some foreigners who are not exactly sure what they are there to do in the first place. The book is largely anecdotal and interesting for that. It almost totally lacks analysis, which one would have expected from a professional writer like the author. You can almost breathe the air in Phnom Penh while reading this book, you can feel high, but I am not sure how much you understand... but there are other books for that. If you are not a young and slightly nut westerner but would like to experience Cambodia like if you were one... this book is for you!! :-)

(Off the Road in Phnom Penh, by Amit Gilboa, Asia Books, 2000.)

Dinner at Pam Lok and disco

The chubby owner recalled how during what he called "the communist times" the restaurant already existed but only had four or five tables and very little choice of ingredients and dishes, if any. When I asked him, he said by "communist times" he meant up to 1993, when Cambodia once again became a monarchy. Of course, he knows that the king only wields nominal authority and the real levers of power are the hands of the government, in large part the heir of the communists who ruled even after the Khmer Rouge abandoned the capital and hid in the jungle. "The Communists", really, are still running the country today, in 2002.

I could count perhaps twenty tables and the choice of appetizers and main courses was enormous. To make things easier on non-Khmer speakers (the restaurant is not cheap for average Cambodians, but we saw both local and foreign patrons) the available choices were presented in a fat photo-album: under each photograph – there were two per page – the dish was explained in Khmer, French and English and the price was given for small, medium and large portions. Take your pick!

It was late in the evening and most other patrons were finished and on their way out, so there was a surplus of staff and each of us was waited upon by two or three petite and smiling waitresses in white shirts. They must have been in their late teens or early twenties. Just like their male colleagues, who took care of our drinks, bread, etc. they exuded a sparkling *joie de vivre* which betrayed their relative immunity to the horrors of the recent history of their country. They were all born after the end of the Khmer Rouge regime in 1979 and although they had lived all their lives in a poor and dictatorial country, they had not experienced the genocide (though surely all of their families had) and could have a reasonable hope for a better future.

After dessert, we were all presented with a real treat: a waitress took position behind each one of us and began and neck and shoulder massage which really was an unexpected and surprising pleasure. I feared this would be reflected in our bill, but it really was not. Not directly at least, though probably in the prices of the food and drinks, and deservedly so. We were happy to pay the bill and give a generous tip.

At the end of the massage session, the owner suggested we go for an evening of dance at a disco, in which it became soon clear he or his company had an interest. I never liked discotheques. I never did and I am pretty sure I never will. In fact I do not like dancing to begin with, any type of dancing, and I detest loud pop music. To be precise, I do not like to dance myself, I do not mind going to a ballet or watching others dance as long as the accompanying decibels stay within the two-digit range.

Few times I went dancing in my life. Once was an adolescent, in the United Kingdom, during a couple of summers spent there learning English, and the only purpose then was to pick up girls on the floor, it was a sort of heavy duty work that I abhorred but had to be done if I wanted to have a chance with the Scandinavian girls I was chasing. It actually worked!

More recently, I went dancing while visiting Russia and Ukraine as a NATO official to discuss political and military cooperation and partnership with the former enemies of the West. After the long formal working sessions, and ensuing vodka-inundated dinners largely based on pork fat, our friendly Russian or Ukrainian interlocutors often would insist on going to a discotheque, and it would have been too rude to refuse – so let us say in those cases I did it for the cause of peace and international cooperation. I carefully avoided any mingling with local beauties lest that became a potential source of blackmail material. And it was fun to see the Russians and Ukrainians dance: mostly the girls danced on the discotheque floor, and the men watched from the sides. So I danced very little anyway. But I am digressing.

In Phnom Penh, I went along only because I was curious to see a Cambodian discotheque and the kind of crowds that would frequent it. I feared they would look just like those everywhere else in the world. I was right, which will probably keep me safely out of further discotheques for a few more years. The general ambience and décor (psychedelic lights and pop music loud enough to prevent conversation) was the same you would find in a discotheque in Toronto, Turin or Taipei; Berlin, Boston or Bombay. Also the absurdly overpriced drinks were the same. The loud side of globalization.

However, one felt more protected here than in an equivalent western establishment: a prominent sign by the door announced that no guns were allowed inside, thus relieving fears of getting caught in the middle of a salsa and merengue shoot-out! No photographs were allowed, either, phew, my privacy was not at risk! When I told him I just wanted to take photos of my friends bouncing like monkeys on the dance floor I had to argue with one of the bouncers who wanted me to leave my camera by the entrance; I was reluctant to part with my Nikon, but had to solemnly promise not to turn it on.

I told him I understood the no-gun policy, but why no photos? The reply was that certain habitual patrons, such as high government officials or foreign diplomats, did not want to see themselves in the pages of the local tabloids in possibly compromising positions or company!

Speaking of the latter, I became slightly suspicious when the restaurant owner offered to let the waitresses come to the discotheque with us. Yet, they were so friendly, it was hard to turn them away, and so we packed as many as would fit in our van and drove to the disco together.

I expected some sort of move on their part, and was nearly certain this was a thinly veiled offer for sexual services to wrap up our sumptuous meal and wild dances. And to top up their earnings and tips. I was wrong. The girls danced with my friends (I did not dance but sat deep in a soft sofa with my switched-off Nikon on my lap, sipping gin and tonic) seemed to have a good time, and when the moment came for us to go back to the hotel they hitched a ride from some reckless driver on a passing motorbike, waved good-bye and went home. I was relieved.

7. Ready for an after-dinner neck and shoulder massage!

6. ALONG THE MEKONG

A gain we were up and running before dawn. At the capital's boat jetty, a few peddlers offered drinks and snacks. One, improbably, had a single copy of the *International Herald Tribune* for sale, the first international newspaper from any country I saw in Cambodia, and the last I would ever be able to lay my hands on for the next several weeks. It also cost twice as much as in Europe. It came from their Bangkok printing press and it was two days old, but I was hungry for international news and did not hesitate to grab it at once.

The presence of the western printed press in Cambodia vaguely reminded me of the good old Soviet times, when everything was censored but I could, occasionally, buy newspapers from "imperialist countries" at the newsstands of international hotels in Moscow. The Soviet regime could tolerate that: few of its citizens would ever have a chance to access and read the subversive stuff – they could not even easily walk into the lobby of these hotels. Even if they did, they would not have the dollars required for the purchase. On the other hand, at least some of the westerners in the hotels would be convinced, and go home telling others, that censorship in the USSR was not that strict after all. Anyway, there was the language barrier that would work as a further filter.

Today all major and many minor newspapers are available on-line and in real time so I guess the whole problem of preventing access to out-of-date printed copies is less relevant for the regime's censors. Fortunately, it is difficult for governments to control access to information on the internet, as recent attempts by the Chinese government testify. It is going to be a cat-and-mouse game in the future, between newspapers and websites trying to spread their words and authoritarian governments trying to prevent them from sharing anything they deem inappropriate, or embarrassing. It is hard to predict how it will play out, but I suspect it will be a long struggle, with ups and downs. Software will be decisive, as access to hardware is already becoming very cheap and easy.

Internet cafes were quite numerous and fairly well equipped with fast computers, at least around Siem Reap and Phnom Penh – much less so in smaller towns, as we will find out later. Connection costs (they vary from café to café but were between one and a bit over two dollars per hour), close to insignificant for a western wallet, though far from cheap for an average Cambodian. Yet many young Cambodians could be seen making use of these services during the cafés' opening hours, which was sometimes pretty much around the clock. Most importantly, as more and more urban Cambodians spoke foreign languages, the internet meant pretty much assured access to independent information the government cannot control. Or so I hoped.

Sailing upstream

Around seven o'clock we boarded the same type of creaky, rusty, floating cigar-tube which we had used from Siem Reap, only a bit smaller. Again I tried and avoid getting packed in the interior cabin with tons of others like anchovies in a tin, and somehow I managed to take position on the upper deck amidst suitcases and motorbikes. After a few minutes we were once more planing over the red oily Mekong, and Phnom Penh disappeared behind the white wake of the cigar-boat's noisy propellers.

Small, lurid settlements of stilt housing interrupted at irregular intervals the thickening jungle that lined either bank of the Mekong. We could distinctly make out people going about their daily lives, chicken and pigs sharing the same premises – and, of course, the same water – for all of their biological requirements. The river tenaciously held its own as it continued to penetrate the thick all-enveloping vegetation, which aggressively protruded toward the water from the edge of the banks as if trying to expand over the space occupied by the flowing liquid. The more we moved upstream, the more the jungle seemed to win the day. The river became imperceptibly narrower and narrower, and its banks gradually came closer and closer to us, increasing our apparent speed and heightening the sensation of being in the wild.

We stopped for a few minutes at some of the more sizable villages along the banks, allowing a few passengers to disembark and others to get on board. Unfortunately, there was no time to go ashore and explore.

At some of the stops, a number of minute adolescent girls hopped on as well. They squatted on the passageway which ringed the boat and tried to sell bottled purified water and delicious French-style baguettes, warm out of the oven. The French did leave something good behind after all. Sometimes exquisite bread-cakes were also on offer as were assorted tropical fruits, wrapped in banana leaves and beautifully displayed on a wide round metal platter which the girls showed off with legitimate pride. Some also had a host of different, and totally unfamiliar, sweet and savory foods which I tried but did not especially appeal to my normally curious palate, yet seemed to be popular with Cambodians.

Some of the girls were still on board when the boat left, and they deftly maneuvered themselves and their wares around people and cargo while the boat was moving at full speed. They disembarked at the next stop, sometimes many kilometers further up the river. I was not sure how they will get back to their village of origin, as there may not be a boat going in the opposite direction until the next day. Maybe they just waited until the next day. But I supposed it made business sense for them as they could keep selling sweets and French baguettes to the many hungry passengers of the ferry.

Suggested reading: River of Time

Between 1970 and 1975 Jon Swain, the English journalist portrayed in David Puttnam's film, "The Killing Fields", lived in the lands of the Mekong river. This is his account of those years, and the way in which the tumultuous events affected his perceptions of life and death as Europe never could. He also describes the beauty of the Mekong landscape — the villages along its banks, surrounded by mangoes, bananas and coconuts, and the exquisite women, the odours of opium, and the region's other face — that of violence and corruption.

He was in Phnom Penh just before the fall of the city to the Khmer Rouge in April 1975. He was captured and was going to be executed. His life was saved by Dith Pran, the New York Times interpreter, a story told by the film The Killing Fields. In Indochina Swain formed a passionate love affair with a French-Vietnamese girl. The demands of a war correspondent ran roughshod over his personal life and the relationship ended.

Jon Swain spent many years in Vietnam, and obviously left his heart there. He was brave, curious and meticulous, indispensable features of a good reporter, especially a war reporter. He was also detached from his grim subject matter and therefore able to keep a balanced and unbiased approach.

He can also be rather disconcerting when he effortlessly hops from one paragraph dedicated to the global consequences of the war to the next paragraph in which he details a brothel in Saigon. But that is part of what makes reading his book fun! He is not a political scientist, and unlike many journalists does not pretend to be one!

This book provides a highly valuable account of the final years of the Vietnam War (Swain was there from 1970 to 1975) and is still highly instructive several decades on.

(River of Time, by Jon Swain, Vintage, 1996.)

Stuck in the mud at Sombok

Finding a hotel was easy, there was one, just in front of the jetty. Here, like most other times during the course of this trip, I would be the only one to whom the local boys would offer to carry luggage. I am not sure whether because my salt and pepper beard made me look older and weaker, or because the others had their back-packs on their shoulders all the time, but my beat-up dark gray hard-shell Samsonite always got picked up and carried up and down whatever obstacle lied between me and a bed, be it a muddy embankment or a steep staircase.

I did not mind that at all, of course. Some fellow travelers made fun of my wheeled Samsonite. They would struggle along with their cool but heavy backpacks on their shoulders; the latest models were so pretty that they were protected from rain and dust by an outer sac which however made it impossible to use the shoulder straps and thus became absolutely impractical to carry. I found that wheels and handles made my hard-shell safer to use for rough travel since I could keep anything in it without risking breakage (think of my bone opium pipes!), soaking or soiling. I had not factored in the added bonus of its serious official appearance that prompted all those spontaneous offers to carry it, but I would keep that in mind for the next time I must buy a piece of luggage!

A boy, about fourteen, who seemed to be in charge of the family run hotel (his parents were away) and whose name I forgot, spoke simple English, but had mastered an excellent pronunciation. Unsurprisingly, he had never travelled to an English speaking country. I concluded that television does produce positive results every now and then.

Rest of the day walking around Sombok, which was not much to write home about. One of a long list of villages which lived off fishing and subsistence agriculture, kids playing in the mud and dish antennas providing a hook to the world.

Early in the morning we tried and visit the Sombok monastery, the main cultural interest in Kratie, but it was about 10 kilometers out of town and in this rainy season it might have been risky to get there – the Mekong was near its high-water mark, and the white-board which is updated daily near the gas station did not indicate any improvement for the next day or two. We might be delayed, we might miss the boat to continue our trip toward Laos. But we had no choice, it was now or never, off we went. There would be another boat tomorrow.

After some negotiations with a taxi driver, six of us decided to take on rain and possible floods and give it a try. As we moved out of Kratie, the road took us through a series of hamlets, mostly on stilts. The latter were actually proving their worth, as the ground below was completely flooded, and so were the rice fields which began just behind the hamlets and continued as far as the eye could see. As usual, people, especially children, were friendly and cheerful. The dirt road, all things considered, was in pretty good shape. Traffic was almost nonexistent, except for the omnipresent motorcycles growling to and fro – not an insignificant exception as we would soon find out.

After driving for several kilometers our driver made a right turn and the road suddenly become much rougher, the mud was deeper and pretty soon we are stuck. We pushed the taxi out of its hole but the driver refused to go on. No monastery today.

We got out of the taxi and walked a bit further to explore, but the road suddenly ended a few hundred meters further; a reinforced concrete bridge was in the making to pass over a flooded area but it was nowhere near to being finished. No one was at work on the site. There would still be a way to go to the monastery by wading the flooded field in front of us, under and around the bridge-to-be. Judging from some Cambodians we saw doing just that, we would have water up to our knees, but we hesitated and time was short, we could miss our boat to Stung Treng. To be honest, I am not sure I would have waded anyway, even if we had had the time, at the risk of leeches and infections. We felt a bit silly and were surely disappointed but this is the kind of setbacks one must factor in the trip when traveling in the tropical jungle during the monsoon season...

Back to our waiting taxi, we were resigned to head back to Kratie, or so we thought. Not a minute after we slammed the door of the vehicle shut, we are stuck in the mud again. Now all of us got out and tried to help pushing the vehicle back and forward. At one point it looked as if it could make it, we all jumped on board again but the driver steered dangerously close to the of curb of the road and one wheel was about to hang over the edge. Some five meters below, the sight of a muddy ditch made my heart pump just a bit too fast for comfort. Trying to stay calm, I proposed we all get off the taxi with some haste. The taxi was stuck again, and it refused to come out of the hole in which its spinning wheels had confined it. We had no more time to waste, or we would miss our boat. So we paid the driver and left him then ran back to the main road to catch some motorcycles and hitch a ride back to "town".

I felt sorry for the driver, I really did not want to leave him there, but after consulting with my friends we agreed we had no choice. Nothing we could do here anyway. The best was to go back to the pier, where we could alert someone to go and help, perhaps with another vehicle to tow the taxi out of the mud.

On the way back, again we passed by the peaceful hamlets we had seen earlier. My driver, unsurprisingly, liked to ride his bike quite fast, it was fun but I had to hold on tight to him for dear life, and to my cameras. Then, when we got to Kratie, he inexplicably stopped at some shop along the way, to make a phone call! We were short of time and I became a bit impatient, but he had a good reason: as we spoke no Khmer and they could not utter a word of any of our multiple European languages they had not idea where we wanted to go!

So the shopkeeper, who spoke some English, translated and wished us a happy journey, after which we were, finally, on our way to rejoin the rest of the group and our baggage and could hop onto the boat to Stung Treng. We could only hope our unlucky driver was able to get his taxi off the hole after all, and I feel sorry we were not more helpful and had to leave him there. We left some extra money for him at our hotel with a local guide who knew him.

Suggested Reading: River's Tale

From windswept plateaus to the South China Sea, the Mekong flows for three thousand miles, snaking its way through Southeast Asia. Long fascinated with this part of the world, former New York Times correspondent Edward Gargan embarked on an ambitious exploration of the Mekong and those living within its watershed.

The River's Tale is a rare and profound book that delivers more than a correspondent's account of a place. It is a seminal examination of the Mekong and its people, a testament to the their struggles, their defeats and their victories.

Gargan completed an ambitious project: to travel along the whole course of one of the world's longest rivers (the 12th longest) for a year, exploring the nature, the cultures and the economic activity that takes places on its banks and hinterland.

He does remarkable job of observing what happens around him and narrating a captivating story. He is humble enough not to pass judgement, but he does make interesting observations on history, economics and politics when he sees things happening around him.

A remarkable account of traveling in a region spanning several countries which share a great river!

(River's Tale – One year Along the Mekong, by Edward Gargan, Vintage Books, 2003.)

River life at Stung Treng

The daily smaller cigar-tube fast boat up the Mekong, from Kratie to Stung Treng, does not leave early in the morning unlike all the others we have taken so far. It waits for the bigger cigar-tube which arrives from Phnom Penh around noon, so that those who so wish can transfer from one boat to the other and do the whole trip from Phnom Penh to Stung Treng in one day.

When the boat from the capital moored at the pier, around noon, we were ready to proceed north. The boat today was smaller than the ones we used so far; same cigar-tube shape, same freezing air-con, same lack of open windows, same only-one-door at the front of the cabin, same filthy toilet, just smaller. Even the seats, packed as tight as humanly possible, seemed smaller; I am anything but a big man, but I barely fit in my place. In addition, for some reason, we were unceremoniously told we had to take our seat inside, no seating on the top deck allowed. Which was just as well, as it was raining pretty hard.

The cabin was booked solid, virtually every seat was taken by people and cargo. OK the chances of anything happening on a calm river ride were small, but if we had a problem this boat would become a mass grave in no time. Again I counted on statistics being on my side, we only had to take this boat once! The TV set started playing a kung-fu video, and the volume was turned all the way up. Some of the Cambodians on board seemed to enjoy it, most others try to doze off; a few passed food and drinks around. Very few chatted, a sort of uneasy silence pervaded the cabin. I was quite uncomfortable in my tiny and hard seat, and decided to challenge both our orders and the icy rain and go and sit outside on the cabin's roof.

Like everything else on this boat, the passageway around it was smaller too, and so were the hand rails I had to hold on to walk from the door near the bow toward a free spot amidship on the roof. In the end, half a dozen of us found a way to sit down between a motorcycle and various other trunks and cases. It rained pretty intensely, and the boat's speed made each fat raindrop hit my face like a bullet. Nevertheless, it was more pleasant and refreshing to be out here in the open than stuffed in the noisy belly of the cigar-tube watching to kung-fu.

We had now left the last major town of Cambodia behind us and were following the Mekong as it was cutting through a rural area closer to the Laotian border. The land route was still not entirely safe and stories of hold-ups and even assassinations of tourists continued to discourage overland travel between Cambodia and Laos, but on the river we were, or at least we felt, safe. The Mekong invited us again toward its deeper recesses. Our floating cigar-tube penetrated one more time, with inexorable determination, the thick jungle.

The poor hamlets, witnesses of a stubborn human will to conquer this all-swallowing nature, became fewer and farther between. Sometimes just a house or two dotted the deep dark green vegetation. The further we sailed upstream, the narrower the river became, and we were now so close to both river banks that we could distinctly make out scenes of everyday life ashore. Women doing the laundry, children frolicking, some chicken picking food from the ground.

We could even make eye contact with the curious inhabitants. Each wave of their hands was both a warm, cheery welcome and a melancholy, definitive adieu. I could not help but wonder: what were we looking for among these hospitable strangers? What was the point of my being here, as I could not speak with them and anyway would in all likelihood never even see them again? How much more did I understand after this quick passing through? And yet I was convinced that even this tenuous connection did make for some communication, and therefore did help me absorb just a bit more the reality of this country.

Landfall in Stung Treng, which means the "river tree" was in the late afternoon. The bow of our cigar-tube gently closed in on the muddy and steep slope of the river bank. The usual wooden plank was laid down and passengers began to disembark, keeping their precarious balance as the boat crew helped them to the firm ground; after that, it was a dozen meters of uphill steps in the mud to the road. A few boys working for the local guesthouses eagerly approached the foreigners, they brandished their bilingual English-Cambodian business cards (sometimes trilingual, in Chinese as well) and offered to help carry our luggage while trying to persuade us their guesthouse really was the best in town.

As soon as we were on the ground we had an emergency. A tourist from Milan has dislocated his shoulder and is suffering extreme pain.

The boys from the guesthouses scurried around looking for a doctor, but none was at hand. After an hour or so, someone showed up saying they found a friend of a friend who once did perform the painful maneuver to replace someone's shoulder. He was available to try and do it again. It was not very reassuring, but it was as good care as the poor fellow was going to get, and the unfortunate tourist, who could hardly move in his condition, had no choice, and accepted the offer. In the evening I would see him again at our guesthouse and he looked much better, the friend of the friend did know what he was doing and the shoulder was back in its place; it still hurt but come morning he would be all right. Phew!

Assault guns and porn posters

The last leg of the Mekong ride in Cambodia was the most adventurous. There was no scheduled public service from Stung Treng to the border with Laos. In fact, until very recently this border post was not officially open at all except to border trade between local Lao and Cambodian residents, though stories abounded that anyone willing to fork out the necessary tips to the border guards would be let through. Why was I not surprised?

The only way forward was to rent our own fast boats, two pirogues, each powered by what must be the world record holders for noise level produced by marine outboards. Their bulky engine blocks were installed at about one-third of the boat's length from the stern, and their shaft extended backward, almost horizontally, for several meters from the rearmost tip of the stern, until the small and flimsy two-blade propeller sank, just, below the water level. This design serves the skippers well in the dry winter season, when the Mekong's water level is at its lowest, and every centimeter that can be shaved from the boat's draft counts.

The roaring churn of the props produced a feisty white wake, whose shape resembled that of a giant cock's tail and shot foam up into the air for at least a good couple of meters. The frequent inevitable cavitation, as the skipper struggled to keep the blades underwater, added to the mayhem of the unmuffled exhausts, but it all made for an adrenaline pumping ride. A fresh wind slapped the boat's spray on our bodies and faces, which was fine, we were used to it by now, but I had to take extra care for my cameras and lenses, their electronics would not have enjoyed a shower, not even a picturesque one like this. My $1 poncho from Phnom Penh was put to the test!

We proceeded for a bit over an hour, and our two boats seemed to be the only ones heading for the border this morning. The landscape was quiet and flat. Only a small village or two on our way, and the rest of the banks were almost completely uninhabited. A few local boats cruised by, their occupants looking at us rather perplexed.

Then, without any prior warning, the skippers steered to port and we made landfall on a muddy embankment, which at first looked no different from any of the many other muddy embankments we had come across. I looked around and, some fifty meters inland, a shiny Cambodian flag was flying on a rather disconsolate mast, a telltale sign of officialdom, and behind it there was a rickety house on stilts which had to be the Cambodian border post.

We disembarked, passed by the flag pole and a goat which meekly tried to come closer to meet us but was prevented from doing so by a very short leash tied to a tree, and climbed the steps up the stilt house and into the offices. The house itself was comprised one office and three bedrooms, plus a pleasant verandah with a river view where we could sit down and await for instructions. The smiling Cambodian border officers were smartly dressed in their green uniforms and quite polite. We handed over our passports and three of them got on with their busy work of stamping, registering, again stamping, stapling, etc.

Meanwhile, I looked around and noticed that in one of the bedrooms three Kalashnikovs and one M-16 machine gun stood neatly lined up on a rack, while a couple of posters of naked women adorned the otherwise austere wood paneled walls above them. One of the ladies in the nude looked like some sort of Madonna, halo and all! Most border stations I had seen around the world would have a photo of the president, or a monarch, or perhaps a past leader whom the nation universally recognized as a kind of father figure. But I must say I enjoyed the posters, they made for a less dramatic border crossing and told volumes about what was important for young men the world over.

The atmosphere was relaxed, the guards were clearly in a good mood, so I instinctively reached for my camera and armed my flash unit, but was held back by Roberto, who was monitoring the stamping and stapling, and who sternly admonished me not to even think about taking pictures like that, at least not until we had all received our passports back and were cleared to leave the country.

After a good twenty minutes or so our passport were ready. The commanding officer checked them one more time, counted them and smiled brightly as he handed them back to us and ...asked for a tip. Just like that, he said, could you please give a tip for the officers. How much? Two dollars per person — per passport, that is, not per officer.

I smiled back and said this was too much, we were poor budget travelers, and proposed one dollar per person, and the tour leader free, just like the travel agents do, for a total of ten dollars. The commandant quickly agreed, we shook hands and I complimented them for their meticulous stamping work.

After we put our passports securely back in our pockets I approached one of the officers and told him how I was really impressed with the way they keep their weapons so neatly on their rack, and would he like to pose for me in front of his arsenal? He was manifestly quite flattered and after a quick questioning glance toward the commandant, who nodded back, he agreed to pose with the Kalashnikovs, the M-16 and the porn posters. The latter was really the main reason why I wanted to take the photo, of course, but that will remain a secret. We headed back to the pirogues. Adieu Cambodia.

One more minute of slow crossing and we were at the border post on the Laotian side. This was a much more spartan arrangement than their Cambodian counterpart. A small office on stilts sheltered two officers, but no machine guns, no elaborate registry and no porn posters. The guards were stone-faced and curt. They looked through our passports, stamped what they had to stamp and then dryly asked for a tip, much the same way an airline clerk would ask for a boarding pass at an airport gate if you are late for your plane and everyone is already on board. Again Roberto and I engaged in some negotiation to reduce the extortion, paid up and we were welcome to Laos.

8. Along the Mekong

Dolphins, monks and waterfalls

Sabaidi! (*suh-bye-dee!* ie Hi! Ciao!) The most onomatopoeic phrase of any language I do not speak! We would hear it and speak it hundreds of times over the next few weeks and every time it sounded new, sweet, alive. The first time we heard it is at the first frontier village, just meters from the Cambodian border, where our pirogues dropped us before quickly turning back.

The first occupation of our visit to Laos was to look for Mekong's famous fresh-water dolphins. Their numbers were down because of the increase of motor boats, we were told, but they were still around and an interesting curiosity. I confess I did not now there was such a thing as a river dolphin. We walked around a bit to try and see them from the shore, then we took the offer of a local to go looking on a small boat, a very slow one this time. After maybe ten minutes we did see a small pod of dolphins, maybe half a dozen of them. They came out to breath quickly, we could barely see their blowhole, and showed us their tail when they dove back underwater. Cute. Not quite as much fun as ocean-going dolphins which jump way out of the water and do not fear the dive boats I often see them from, but this was different and interesting.

We walked around after a quick lunch by the riverside and the atmosphere was distinctly more relaxed and easygoing than in any Cambodian village we have seen. As we were near the border crossing, we were obviously not the first visitors they ever saw, though since the crossing was restricted to Laotians and Cambodians until very recently they may not have encountered all too many pale western faces. Swarms of children, mixed with piglets and cocks, paraded around and curiously (the children!) peeped with astonishment into the viewfinder of my zoom lens.

At dinner in Muang Khong, we started a conversation with a soft spoken obviously Anglo-Saxon man who was eating by himself. I asked to join him at this table. Peter was German. He was actually Bavarian, as he made it a point to specify. He had been riding his motorbike (a BMW, of course, how silly of me to ask) from London and was on his way to Singapore. In the spring he was "made redundant" at his financial firm in the City, given a golden handshake and set free. Now master of his own life again he sat down to think what to do with it. So he decided to take time off before getting back into the rat race. Sounded quite familiar!

As he had always been an avid biker he thought of driving across France, Italy, Greece, Turkey, Iran, Pakistan, India, Burma, Thailand,

Laos, Cambodia, back to Thailand, Malaysia and Singapore, from where he would ship his bike back and hop on a plane home. He had had a smooth ride so far, except for some not so friendly Kurds in Turkey – Kurds don't especially love Germans as so many Kurds live in Germany and have a hard time getting a passport even after many years of residence, even if they were actually born there, have never been to Turkey and German is their only language.

He also said the Laotian border officials wanted "tips", but he got through without paying any. And how did he do that? I was a bit envious since we have just been victims of tip extortions ourselves. Simple, he said, he just refused to pay and after seven or eight hours they relented and let him through. Now, that is what you call true German resolve! I refrained from asking him whether he thought wasting seven or eight hours of his time at the border post was worth a few dollars, it would have been beyond the point... We shared a few good Beerlao – a truly good beer which will become a constant presence at our tables – and wished him a safe trip. Tomorrow he would be at the same Laotian border post we went through, and after that the Cambodian officers with the guns and porn posters in the bedroom will take their turn. If he insisted not to pay their tips he might end up spending a long time in the region.

In the morning, after sharing a breakfast of banana cakes, I wished him good luck, he was going to need it, and we were on our way, in a small van, direction Pakse

Pakse was really nothing to write home about, but an unavoidable hub to get to Northern Laos. We spent a few daylight hours and one night there. Late in the afternoon Renata and I were walking around looking for an internet café, without much success, when we walked by a buddhist temple. We went in and saw that all was quiet but something was in the making, the young monks and novices were scurrying to and from in the courtyard, and after a few minutes a gong went off. I ran to the guesthouse, only a few hundred meters away, and I was soon back with my personal photographic arsenal.

By this time all monks were assembled for the evening prayers and as soon as everyone was seated they began their cavernous deep singing of Buddhist mantras. It was a moving atmosphere, in part because it was the first time for me. Many young boys in Laos get a religious education in the monasteries in their teens. It is part of their culture if not necessarily, these days, of their religious convictions.

9. Young monk in Laos

7. NEW AND ANCIENT CAPITAL

Early rise and transfer to the small nondescript airport. Uneventful flight to Vientiane, the rather plain looking capital city. We checked-in at our hotel and I took a walk around the city.

Vientiane reminded me of Tirana, in Albania, the way it was some ten years ago, the last time I visited. Everything was falling apart, broken, neglected, dirty. There was no charm in grey blocks of apartment buildings and littered streets. Economic activity was minimal, at least at a first cursory look.

On the positive side, some older buildings, probably dating back to the colonial past, were on a small, human scale, everywhere was within walking distance. Tirana has improved a lot since then, I hope Vientiane does too.

Chicken and wine

A wine shop just a couple of doors from the hotel was perhaps one of the single most surprising sites in Laos. It was a gently air-conditioned, softly lit shop, with a very pretty multilingual Lao lady working at the counter and eager to step up and explain the most detailed nuances about French wines. In a way this shop was a cultural shock, given the context in which it is located. However, come to think of it, it was a shock only inasmuch as I assumed that in poor Laos there would be no chance of finding a good shop with excellent wines. Worse, if I subconsciously assumed that no one could possibly want this expensive wine in a 300-dollar-a-year salary population. The cute lady proposed I buy a bottle of *Dom Perignon* champagne, 1990 vintage, for that price!

In fact, it should be quite normal for a capital city, albeit of a small country, to have at least one good wine shop, should it not? Not everyone in a poor if the country is poor, of course, and in a capital city there are the embassies, foreign visitors, etc. all of whom can afford expensive wines and as far as the the Lao state is concerned this activity of course generates a revenue in the form of income and excise taxes from the sales, plus a few jobs in commerce, distribution, etc.

I spent the whole afternoon walking around downtown Vientiane under heavy monsoon rain. I could confirm that the town was pretty well run down by years of neglect. A few traditional constructions stood side by side with dreary government office buildings, many built in the sixties and seventies and obviously never properly maintained. Vientiane had a human dimension which one rarely finds in a capital city. Even the most powerful ministries are made up of two or three story buildings which look more like villas than ministerial buildings.

Vientiane lies on the left bank of the Mekong, and it faces Thailand, but when I went to the waterfront to have a look it was raining hard and the mist was so thick that one could see absolutely nothing on the other side.

I walked into one of the many internet cafes that have opened up in central Vientiane. A couple dozen computers were neatly lined up and a good half of them were taken by an Italian group, who judging by their conversation must have been spent most of the afternoon in here. Some of them were playing a chess game online against an opponent who was lord-knows-where in the world! Now, who would come all the way to Vientiane, of all places, to sit down at an internet café and play electronic chess! But they were too busy for me to intrude and ask…

One of the few imposing buildings in Vientiane is the culture palace, a huge white construction. Again a similarity with Tirana, where Skanderbeg square remains the most ostentatious architectural heritage of the dictatorship of old. By the entrance, a young lady was selling CDs and tickets for the evening performance. She had a stereo system set up on her table and it was blasting some ear piercing pop music at an unimaginable number of decibel, so much so that even if we were in open air I could hardly hear a word of what she was saying.

I had been told some Lao music would be played tonight and had entertained the thought of spending an evening savoring traditional melodies, and when I saw she had a book of tickets to sell I pulled out my wallet in anticipation. Wrong! When the lady finally turned the volume down, she explained that the evening's program consisted of Lao pop singers who would perform the very same songs I was listening to as we spoke. I said thanks but no thanks and left, disappointed.

I later regretted having missed the concert, however. Yes, the music would have been of the same kind of imitation pop culture one often finds in countries where that kind of art was forbidden until recently – again Albania in the mid-nineties came to mind, but Albanian musicians have evolved quite a bit by now. Yet, this is Laos today, and it would surely have been interesting, sociologically if not musically, to attend the event and see a crowd of young Laotians enjoy a pop concert.

My expectation of a traditional music performance was based on obsolete stereotypes some travelers always have when visiting exotic places. I unreasonably expected old Lao music just as I had visited old *wats*. But surely the people of Vientiane cannot be expected to live in their past! They would expect from a concert in their culture hall what any of us would expect in a concert hall in our home town. And yet I was convinced that there could be more attention to local art and less to imitation of foreign stuff, welcome as it may be.

Next morning it was market time: foods, artifacts, Akha necklaces, and lots of cheap imported junk. Not the most interesting market, but it was good to see economic activity stirring up.

In the evening we decided to go and eat at the evening market. We found a smiling lady who was busy grilling chicken. The fragrance was irresistible, and we sat down at a table next to her stand. It was quite delicious indeed and he atmosphere of the evening market allowed me to take the pulse of local life in the capital. The only sore note was the bill, which I realized was not what the locals were paying.

Price were obviously set way higher because we were foreigners, they did not seem to realize this would quickly become counterproductive. They did not understand that they could get away with it once, but we would probably not go and eat there again, and if we did we would negotiate a Laotian price first.

More generally, when word spreads that visitors get ripped off somewhere, the damage can be long lasting. It takes far longer to attract tourists than to lose them, especially in the era of the internet.

Not that this is a problem unique to Laos, far from it. My own country, Italy, is a prime culprit in this respect. How many stories have I heard of foreign visitors being overcharged by some – a minority for sure – Italian restaurants, hotels, taxis, barber shops, etc.? Even if only a few cheat, bad reputation sticks onto the whole country.

And if one is to believe statistics Italy has paid a price for that loss of reputation, slipping consistently down in world tourism rankings. I can only hope that countries which pin their hopes for foreign currency earnings on tourism will not repeat the same mistakes, but from what I have been able to see in my travels it is likely that they will.

Anyway we ate our chicken, which was excellent, but left with a bitter aftertaste when a few children come around asking for our leftovers. Vientiane did not look so poor. As I think back to that moment, I wish I had bought a bit more chicken for the kids. But then again this kind of help is often frowned upon, they say it encourages beggars. It's a hard one to call.

The next day, breakfast at Scandinavian Bakery near the waterfront. Sweden had been a long time friend and donor to Laos, maybe this was why? Or perhaps there were enough Swedish NGOs here that some entrepreneurial local decided to make money catering for them? After cappuccino and croissant, a city tour on tuk-tuk was an exhilarating experience. Drivers like to race each other along the wide boulevards of Vientiane, and thin traffic allows them to test their little growling machines to the limit.

Before heading to the capital's airport, to fly north, to Luang Prabang, we all got another *Seeing Hands* massage and sauna (Turkish bath) at the Red Cross headquarters, herb scent in steam coming from under a wooden shack.

A short hop and we landed at the airport of Luang Prabang (the City of the Golden Buddha), which was small, clean and pleasant: a huge improvement over Vientiane. They must have had a reason to move the capital from the former to the latter, and it'd better have been a good one!

Two wheel for Luang Prabang

The moment we stepped out of the terminal building to look for transportation to town we realized that a young snooty boy in jeans was directing all the *tuk-tuk* (motorized tricycle) traffic, and we would not get a ride unless we dealt with him. He controlled a sort of cartel, so that the fixed price – for foreigners! – was set at 10,000 kip (1 US dollar) per person, whether the *tuk-tuk* would depart with just one passenger or fill up with six. It was annoying to feel impotent in the face of the boy's overbearing behavior, but we had no choice, and anyway the amount of money involved did not justify wasting any more time arguing with him.

Not that this news to me: I had read of taxis in Rome charging Japanese tourists as much as they pay in Tokyo for a taxi ride from Narita (which is about 200 dollars last I heard, about six times what an Italian would pay).

We started looking for a place to stay and landed at the most inappropriately named *Heritage Guesthouse*, which had very little heritage indeed, dark, moldy and damp. We gave it a pass.

We kept looking until we found the *Say Nam* guesthouse, not far from the river, run by a friendly lady who spoke no English but pretty good French. No need to look any further. The hotel was actually the lady's rather large traditional home, she also lived there in a separate wing. Our rooms were very well appointed, with candid white linen and an elegant teapot and cups. Those on the higher floor also had balconies overlooking the forest and the river.

We checked-in and off we went to rent bicycles, one dollar a day, no deposit, no identification papers, it was all done on trust. Bikes are great here: very little traffic, the city is rather flat, and easy to park ;–)

I spent my first few hours just roaming around with no specific destination in mind. I walked into a silk and bamboo shop, and I bought some pretty scarves, one for me and some for gifts: soft, shiny, typical from Laos and easy to carry. After some negotiation I got a 15% discount. A little later I went back to buy a couple more and the smiling saleswoman only agreed to 10% off. Strange way to do business.

After a while I came to the conclusion that I really loved wondering around and getting lost in this fascinating city. I especially liked the traditional Lao-style houses, all made of wood and raised from the ground. They must have been built by rich locals, and were all surrounded by luxuriant tropical vegetation. And flowers, lots of colorful flowers.

Next day, breakfast was at the same Scandinavian bakery I had seen in Vientiane! Globalization... I would have preferred a local breakfast but was not able to find an eatery that offered one. Perhaps locals do not go out for breakfast, tourists do, and most tourists are probably not as curious as they should be, and local businesses cater to them.

Well, I was a tourist too, so I started my classic tourist rounds at the Royal Palace museum. This was the seat of the monarchy when Luang Prabang was the capital of Laos at different times in its history. One curious exhibit here is a piece of moon rock, taken by one of the Apollo missions and donated by the USA. At the time of my visit the many gifts received from abroad were categorized as coming from "socialist" or "capitalist" countries!

Later on I entered into a silversmith shop and photographed some artisans at work. There was actually some interesting local manufacturing here, silk, wood carvings, jewelry. I did not buy any in the end, I did not have a woman in my heart to whom I could gift this. I thought about buying a pretty silver Akha necklace anyway, and just put it aside for a while until the right woman materialized, but decided it was not worth the investment.

I spent the rest of the day with Roberto working out a plan for our upcoming trip to the hill tribes in the north of the country. Because of the difficulty in road transportation during the rainy season we decided to give up Phongsaly, the northernmost destination in our original plan, and head straight north along the Mekong and the Nam Ou rivers, and then due west by bus toward Muang Sing.

In the evening, a well-deserved session of massage at the Red Cross Massage Center, followed by a great natural Turkish bath powered by wood and intensely scented with herbs from the surrounding forests. We were joined by some Israelis. Young kids traveling for a year before they started their military service. They told us it is a common thing to do, one year of freedom around the world before the demanding duty of armed service in their troubled country.

Suggested reading: Mother's beloved

The author is one of the most prominent contemporary writers in Laos. His stories are animated with Laotian virtues of simplicity, compassion, respect for age, and other village mores; they breathe with a gentleness that is fresh and distinctive. Outhine is interested in his own memories, in how to behave with compassion, and in the chain of life among men and women that reaches into the earth.

This book presents fourteen of Outhine Bounyavong's short stories in English translation alongside the Lao originals, marking his formal debut for an American audience. It is also the first collection of Lao short stories to be published in the English language.

A unique collection to understand Lao culture. Oral history which would otherwise be lost can be preserved here. There is also a useful introduction to contemporary Lao literature, and the role of writers during the various periods of monarchy, war and communism of the XX century.

(Outhine Bounyavong: Mother's Beloved, U. of Washington, 1999.)

A fistful of rice for the orange robes

One of my goals in Luang Prabang was to be at sunrise on top of the Phousi mountain to take a few good dawn shots of the city and its surroundings. I had set the alarm clock for a quarter to five in the morning, but as it often happens to me when something important is at stake I woke up just a few minutes before it went off. How our internal clock can be so precise it is difficult for me to fathom. I was immediately awake and fully alert. I was not tired, despite the hour and the long transfers of the previous days.

The sky was heavily clouded, not the best photo weather at all, to put it mildly. I realized there would be no chance for the Phousi I had been planning for, it will have to be on the next trip to Luang Prabang. I was disappointed, and the temptation to go back to sleep and wait for a civilized eight o'clock breakfast was a powerful one. However, I was up now and when I heard the irresistible call of the gong from the Wat Xieng Muang next door my mind was quickly made up and I decided to go look for the monks doing their begging rounds, a daily routine but always an intense moment to witness. In a minute I was out in the street and began looking around, and listening.

Sure enough, the moment I stepped on to Sisavangong road I found myself just at the head of a long line of orange robes which stretched as far as the eye could see in the direction of the temples at the far east of the city's peninsula. They walked in a formation of two distinct groups that were separated by just a few meters so in the distance they actually look like just one very very long line.

Each group was organized in a precise hierarchical order, with the senior monks at the head, followed by progressively younger ones, while the novices trailed at the end. They walked in unison, at a brisk clip but with no hurry. The older monks looked serious, almost solemn as they led the way. The younger ones were more relaxed, some even let out a smile or two.

The itinerary that the monks follow every day runs down from the various temples in the East along Sisavangong, then right at the Royal Palace toward the river and right again along the Mekong left bank all the way back up to the temples. Every twenty or thirty meters, small groups of faithfuls, in twos, threes, or fours, kneeled down on some cushion by the roadside. Each held a cane basket full of sticky rice. As each monk or novice stepped up and lifted the lid of his bowl, they dropped a fistful of rice in it; the lid was then replaced until the next drop.

The spotless bright orange robes radiated an almost incandescent shimmer in the tenuous early morning lights, at a time when everything else was still under a patina of gray mist. My impression was mixed. On the one hand, the choreography was highly suggestive of religious mystery and impenetrable tradition. On the other hand, this was one of the most routine procedures in the Buddhist world, done time and again in countless cities and basically just a way to collect rice for the monks' simple diet. It was special for us foreigners, but not for the Lao.

Despite the early hour, I was not the only foreigner who came to see the procession. About a half dozen of us, armed to the teeth with cameras, telephoto lenses and strobes, buzzed around each way-point on the monks' itinerary and flooded the scene with camera shutters clicking, motorized winders whirring and electronic flashes blasting each time a fistful of rice was dropped in a rice bowl. As the two groups moved along, the photographers ran ahead of them (and of each other) to take positions ahead of the next rice drop. Sometimes I had to walk awkwardly backward to try to get that perfect monk shot. Once I climbed dangerously on the fence of a large house, others jumped on top of benches to get a higher angle on our orange subjects. During the high tourist season, in the winter, the number of photographers could be approaching that of the monks, or more!

Sometimes I wondered whether it would make for more interesting pictures if it were the monks taking photos of visitors rather than the other way around. In fact, I did not just wonder, I did take some photos of the clumsier ones among my peers, and I think I would have been pretty funny myself if anyone had bothered to notice.

A critical "eternal romantic" told me Christians would not appreciate being photographed during Mass, and in fact many churches forbid it. He argued we should likewise respect the monks and leave them alone during their begging rounds. I thought that parallel was not warranted. For one thing, the begging round is not a sacred ceremony, though undoubtedly a serious observance. But I believe to refrain from taking photos would be an excess of self-criticism which one often finds in western eternal romantics, part of their general attitude to leave the world alone as much as possible, even if it means reducing mutual contacts and knowledge. The monks clearly did not object to photographers; actually, the younger ones on a number of occasions displayed a curious interest and smiled at the lenses. They could object if they wanted to, they could let it be known that this was not on and that would be that. But they don't.

After the monks went back to their monastery I was hungry, and decided to go back to the reliable Scandinavian Bakery. It was still early, and I had a full day around town by bike in front of me. It was a pleasant and easy town to savor at leisure. Just before sunset I walk up the steps of the hill of Phou Si monastery, from which one can enjoy a spectacular view over the whole valley and the Mekong.

In the evening I bought a ticket to an interesting performance of traditional dances at the Royal Palace Museum. Virtually all the public was made up of tourists. I sneaked to the front to take some good shots of the adolescent dancers who lightly move across the stage, backed by the rhythmic music of middle aged drummers sitting on the side. A French woman complained that I was in her way and she has paid extra for a front seat! Oh well... anyway I tried not to *déranger la dame* and kept shooting. Especially the girls. They were all very photogenic, their gold, blue and red costumes moving elegantly as their hands and backward-bent fingers draw delicate loops in the air.

The dances were followed by another, smaller show in the gardens of the museum. Some muscular artists from the Akha ethnic minority performed a few numbers to demonstrate strength and dexterity, such as lifting a large bronze vessel full of water by clenching its rim in their teeth!

Dinner was at a small restaurant frequented by local patrons, we were the only foreigners. Once again loud trash music spoiled the atmosphere. I asked the waiter for Lao music and got some sort of very un-Lao pop cacophony which clearly aimed at imitating western disco equivalents. I was disappointed, but once again I told myself I should not have been, this is the music of Laos today, this is the music people here like to listen to. Why do visitors expect to listen only to old music? As if visitors to Italy refused to accept anything beyond "Oh Sole Mio!", ie traditional Italian music from over a hundred years ago. In fact, then and now, when I recall the kind of music that is normally offered in Italian restaurants, it sounds rather pathetic, it is not Italy...

10. Traditional Lao dances

11. Sunrise procession to receive alms

8. AGAINST THE CURRENT ON THE NAM OU

Again up at dawn, at seven o'clock we were at the Luang Prabang ferry harbor on the Mekong, just a five minute walk from our guesthouse.

We had a fundamental choice to make that would impact on the style of our sailing in the next few days: Roberto recommended a slow boat (long wooden pirogue powered by a little diesel engine puttering along at less than 10 km/h against the current) over a fast one (smaller boats powered by a large engine and capable of planing at perhaps 40-50 km/h). I could not agree more.

We had planned our trip to travel against the current, from south to north. It would take longer, of course, to cover any given distance going upstream than it would sailing downstream. But it would give us a much better chance to savor the landscape, feel the water under the hull of the pirogue, and enjoy a gentle breeze on our face.

By 8 o'clock everything had been loaded up and we were off in no time. As we left the last houses of Luang Prabang behind us, our slow boat began to claw its way against the placid current of the Mekong. Soon, there was only virgin jungle all around us. The impenetrable rainforest, painted of wide dark green brush strokes, covered the slopes on both banks and tumbled down decisively, all the way into the water, from the steep cliffs that were marking the Mekong's course.

A few houses, sometimes on stilts, occasionally interrupted our view of the bush and suddenly come into view. On this stretch, the river was flat and quiet, no apparent current, no boulders to break its flow. Its dense clay-like water gently parted as we slided forward along the left bank.

After a good hour we reached the caves of Pak Ou, which were actually a bit disappointing. A small, intimate temple with a myriad statues crammed together. To my inexpert eye, the sculptures there were no match for what we have seen in Luang Prabang, there were too many people and too little space.

When we left the caves the boat took a sharp turn to starboard and we abandoned the Mekong to continue our trip up its tributary, the Nam Ou. We were greeted by an immediate and drastic change of landscape.

The Nam Ou River's span was predictably much narrower than that of the Mekong, and the deep green of the jungle which had framed our course until now was replaced by dramatic vertical rocky cliffs. These dropped several hundred meters straight down into the water, and starkly marked the junction of the two rivers as a monumental post. The Nam Ou was perfectly flat and its water looked absolutely still, as if frozen, with only a few minute ripples reflecting silvery shades, barely breaking the compact glossy brick-red coat of the surface.

Opium pipes and TV antennas

The village to which our skipper had decided to take us was ready and set for the incoming tourists. I tried to ask the skipper its name, but there was no answer. I looked around, no signs. I later looked on all my maps, only some vague references to the area, I think we were somewhere around Pakxeuang, but I am not sure. And I did not even try to pronounce the word.

Smiling ladies sitting behind small their wooden tables displayed their wares and politely invited us to examine various artifacts and cloths. I bought an opium pipe made of cow bone. I would never smoke it, I knew that, but the shape and engraving were endearing to me and I liked the thought of giving a small incentive to honest artisans who used local raw materials and helped preserve ancient skills. A few men were working with a scalpel, they were trying to carve out a tree trunk to make a canoe, but their attitude made me think it was all staged for effect, they somehow did not look like carpenters or coopers but rather actors on a stage. Maybe I was wrong.

A completely different story awaited us at the next village, a few kilometers upstream, again no official name was there to be learned. This time we saw a few houses on stilts and asked the skipper to make a landing. The inhabitants were friendly and immediately welcomed us, but it was abundantly clear that they did not expect a visit on this day! A few children approached and wanted to play, but most of the adults just kept going at their daily routines, weaving, washing, sawing bamboo. A couple of adolescents were curious of Roberto's camera and approached him to peek through his telephoto lens, and had a ball when they did! Their interest turned into elation when they looked through my "fish-eye" wide-angle lens: all of a sudden they could see their own feet and at the same time the top of the sky in the same frame!

It was lunch time and I was hoping for some local delicacy but at a food stall we saw only all imported and mostly junk food, except Lao Beer, and not even that was local, we were told the brewery had been bought by a Thai company. I was rather disappointed but there was no time to go and look around for anything else. It was hot and we were all thirsty and hungry! I gobbled something out of a plastic wrapper and quickly forgot what it was.

Satellite dishes were clearly visible on some of the roofs, almost ostentatiously. One of my companions commented that this was really too bad, television would for ever spoil the gentle and innocent character of these peoples. They would be bombarded with useless commercials and would soon want all kinds of things they did not need. They would see a distorted representation of the world's reality outside their village. Children would spend hours sitting in front of their TV sets and stop socializing and playing outside.

I could not disagree with him more. Let me be clear: I don't watch TV personally, I don't like it, I don't like the idea that I have to watch what they want me to watch, when they want me to watch it. I am convinced the average quality of TV programs ranges from low to terrible.

Yet, it seemed to me that the information and education that an otherwise isolated population could receive through the airwaves was priceless. Yes, it would change their lifestyle as it has changed ours. And I was not sure even about that, this generation was moving fast away from TV and toward the internet anyway. But how on earth could one wish these people did not have this channel of communication available to them was beyond me. The explanation was a silly, selfish desire to preserve "genuine" populations, isolated from western cultural "contamination", so as to be able to come here and photograph "real" Laos. I detest TV, long live TV!

12. Discovering a new reality

13. Grandma

14. Father and daughter

A speck of gold in Suptiem

After skillfully steering his way around some swirling current to follow a sharp bend of the river, our skipper veered abruptly to starboard and made landfall on a small island of mud in the middle of the Nam Ou. This location was called Suptiem, our skipper told us, though I could not find it on any map. In the distance further upstream we could make out people crouching by the waterfront but it was not clear what they are up to. We were told we could not disembark any closer to the mainland as the water was too shallow. So, after we are all on the muddy island, the skipper used some planks to make a bridge to the shore and we started walking toward the crouching people.

As it turned out they were all women, many with their children playing around, but no men in sight. The women had big pans in their hands and they were panning for gold! One proudly showed us a tiny gold leaf she had found earlier in the morning. About one hundred of them worked side by side along the beach. Some were digging a few meters inland, and then sifted carefully through the mud in search of the glittering stuff. It was noon and the tropical sun, having finally broken through the cloud that had blanketed the sky for several days, was shining with all its might, its hot rays hitting heavily on my naked and nearly hairless head, silly me I left my hat on the boat, I would never make this mistake again.

The Nam Ou displayed its usual brick-red intensity, the same color as the muddy river banks, the sky was a cloudless postcard blue and the deep green jungle thoroughly covered the steep mountainsides all around. Everything in sight was either blue, green or brick-red, three colors that would work well together on a woman's dress. Nature looked so simple, so harmoniously assembled. After several days of sailing up the river we had gained altitude, and the air began to feel cooler, and even thinner.

Leaving the ladies to their work we walked up a slippery mud path toward the village itself. Perhaps they did actually find lots of gold here, because Suptiem was evidently a richer, cleaner village than any other we had seen so far. The houses on stilts were neat and proper, built on a perfectly straight line along either side of the main street. Some embryonic urban planning must have gone into the layout of Suptiem. A shining polished communal water pump (hand powered, alas, no generators!) stood by the road side, and people took turns at showering and filling up bottles for their homes. Curious children, as always, came around asking for pens; they looked quite healthy and clean. Some older ladies intervened and tried to sell their pretty embroidery. I am not sure why I should have been surprised by the good standard of living in a small village in the Laotian jungle, but I was.

Deep down into the heart of darkness

As we continued our fluvial journey toward the north, the boat's tack became uneven. Until now the skipper had kept a steady course and speed, but now he had to carefully negotiate his way among treacherous sandbanks and all kinds of floating debris. Sudden cross currents forced him to zigzag in an apparently haphazard way, now to port and now to starboard.

One minute we could almost touch the vegetation on the right bank, the next we were headed straight toward an inlet on the left bank. The skipper's assistant made me descend from the roof structure where I had climbed in search for better angles for my pictures: with his hands and body he explained we had to lower the boat's center of gravity to make it more stable during the sudden turns... safety first!

As the cruising hours gently went by, the deep green of the jungle all around gradually turned darker and darker. The silvery ripples on the brick-clay river surface turned blue. At dusk, it all quickly took on a light gray patina, which then turned into dark gray. The last pirogues still in the water hurriedly made for home, and the last few children interrupted their frolics in the water and disappeared behind the bush. We were obviously late, our boat should have reached Nong Khiaw by now, but the town was nowhere to be seen.

At one point the large suspended bridge of Muang Ngoy appeared before us. A modern structure, if a bit run down, aesthetically out of context in the otherwise bucolic surroundings, but obviously a great bonus in terms of both time and safety for those who use it. From the bridge, the skipper announced, it was just another hour to our final destination.

At the tropics the sun sets quickly. For another thirty minutes or so, the large white clouds which had gathered above during the late afternoon held on to a sliver of dim sunlight which their western rims reflected down to earth. Then, inevitably, the clouds' contours merged with the black sky. The moon had not risen over the mountains yet and all of a sudden it was pitch black all around: water, jungle, boat, even ourselves, everything was ink black. I must say that I enjoyed this moment because, even though I was crammed in a small boat with a dozen other people, it gave me a sensation of blissful solitude in the midst of some of the wildest nature on the planet. I could not see anything or anybody, and could only hear the boat's propeller and the waves.

Suddenly, the weather deteriorated dramatically and a thunderstorm announced itself with a series of loud roars as a strange hot lateral wind began to pick up and hit the boat from starboard. It blew pungent sand from the river banks onto our faces.

The thick downpour delivered the first chill I experienced since arriving in South East Asia, it felt strange after weeks of uninterrupted sticky heat. We all pulled out sweaters, wind-breakers, anoraks, whatever we had (and thought we would never need) and the skipper ordered the plastic curtains which were rolled up all around the roof of the pirogue to be released and fastened down onto the boat's sides to partially protect us from rain and spray, which made the wind-carried dust stick to our skin. Luckily, all photographic equipment had long been stored away for the day.

At this point we were cruising full speed ahead, deep into a Conradian darkness on our pretty solid but navigation-light-less and radio-less, not to speak of GPS-less, radar-less, horn-less and everything-else-less wooden pirogue. I was not sure we had life vests on board but what I knew for sure was that, even if we did, we would never have been able to find them in an emergency and put them on. Even if we had put them on, what would have happened once we had been in the water, at the current's mercy, was anyone's guess. That by this late hour there was obviously no traffic at all on the river did not make me feel much safer: no one to crash into but also no one to come to our help should we be in need. Nevertheless, it was somehow exhilarating to be there!

We did not speak much at all, but deep inside I was excited. How did the skipper manage both to avoid treacherous submerged boulders and to tame the tricky currents without seeing a thing was a mystery to me. That we did not hit a major invisible floating obstacle, like a log, the kind you can hardly see even in broad daylight was, I am sure, sheer luck! Another hour or so later we finally got a glimpse, out in the distance, of the barely visible neon lights of what by then I wanted to believe was Nong Khiaw, our destination. Which it was!

Lettura consigliata (italiano): Mekong Story

Giornalista e viaggiatore, Massimo Morello presenta questo diario di viaggio nel Sud-Est asiatico lungo il Mekong: dal delta, sul Mar della

Cina, sin quasi alle sorgenti, in un monastero buddhista nell'altopiano himalayano della remota regione del Qinghai.

L'autore narra un percorso sul fiume e dintorni attraverso Vietnam, Cambogia, Thailandia, Birmania, Los, Cina e Tibet, tra foreste, montagne, paludi e valli incantate, piste polverose, sentieri di fango e superstrade, villaggi e metropoli, hotel di superlusso e locande malfamate. Un viaggio che l'autore ha compiuto da solo, in battello, bus, auto, a piedi, in un susseguirsi di avventure e disavventure che gli hanno permesso di osservare più da vicino quella che viene definita la nuova Asia.

Un viaggio di sei mesi lungo un fiume lunghissimo. Anzi un meta-viaggio, dato che il percorso Morello lo ha fatto a varie riprese. Osservatore informato, ci racconta le sue esperienze rendendole rilevanti ed interessanti perché ci aiutano a capire i paesi che visita. Un libro di viaggio ma anche di storia e di politica, di costume e di gastronomia. Un ottimo compagno per chi vuol viaggiare in quelle terre, o lungo quel fiume.

(Mekong Story: Lungo il cuore d'acqua del Sud-Est asiatico, Massimo Morello, Touring Club italiano, 2006.)

Nong Khiaw: power to the people!

When we got there, the docking station was packed solid with various boats, and we had to make landfall a bit further on, under a steep muddy incline just under the verandah of a guesthouse. The boat's wooden plank was laid as usual and Barbara and I were the first to disembark and walked onto the mud looking for shelter for the night. We climbed up the steepish and slippery embankment and were met the owner of the guesthouse above: no problems, there were double rooms available at Kip 10,000 (one dollar) per night.

Half an hour later we were around the dining table of the guesthouse's verandah, overlooking the river – though there was not much to overlook as it was still pitch black all around. The wind and rain had stopped, however, and it was pleasant to taste different kinds of fried river fish with sticky rice for dinner. A few hammocks provided an ideal setting for after dinner conversations al fresco.

As announced by a notice on the wall, at about 10:00 o'clock the generator became silent and all lights went out. The erratic nature of power supply was a recurring theme in our travels these days, and in conversations.

It is amazing how so many villages around Laos, even small towns, only have sporadic and unreliable access to electricity. Often the only source of power are small diesel powered generators, with the obvious inconvenience of noise and air pollution that they produce. The reason why this is amazing is that Laos is a major producer, and exporter, of hydroelectric power. The government exports electricity, most of it to Thailand, to raise cash, but it does not yet think it necessary to provide it to its own people.

In the mid-nineties a fierce debate developed over whether or not additional hydroelectric capacity should be built on the Mekong. Opinions were as polarized among the Laotians as they were, and still are, among foreigners, interest groups and environmental organizations. Again the divide between "eternal romantics" and "modernizers" became apparent.

The former see hydroelectric power as a mortal threat to the environment as well as to the traditional way of life of many hill tribes who must be resettled to make room for the new dam's reservoir.

The latter see new hydropower capacity as a clean source of renewable energy, indispensable for the economic development of the region and a precious source of foreign currency from power hungry Thailand and, increasingly, Vietnam. No one really wants additional fossil fuel power generation, so the real issue at stake is whether or not Laotian villages and towns need a reliable source of electricity.

The answer was not, and still is not only an economic one but rather a political one. Eternal romantics believe that rural communities, and certainly these hill tribes, can live very well thank you very much the way they have lived for centuries, i.e. without electricity. They see the arrival of electricity as a curse which changes – for the worse – their traditional way of life, creating unnecessary demand for electric tools and appliances and making it possible for hordes of tourists to invade.

Modernizers, for their part, consider the need for electricity as a self-evident truth, almost a human right, which is indispensable to raise the standard of living. They argue not over whether, but over how to best provide for it. I can only agree with the modernizers.

Later at night a brilliant full moon rose high in the sky. It highlighted the contours of a few small clouds and cast a pale light over the blacked-out village. Tall palm silhouettes of large trees stood still behind the rooftops. There was nothing whatsoever one could possible do in the village, so I retired to my room.

The manager had given each of us a candle to get around in the night; come to think of it, a dozen candles lying on the floor of wood and rattan constructions was a pretty serious fire hazard, but I persuaded myself that, just as with the sealed fast cigar-tube boats on the Tonle Sap, statistics was on my side: we're only here for one night, it's unlikely we'd have a fire just tonight! So I relaxed, pulled out my diary and jotted down a few notes until all of a sudden the day's fatigue set in and I collapsed for what I naively looked forward to be a good long night's sleep.

The most heavily bombed country

At the crack of dawn a rooster started crowing madly and woke everyone up. He must have been worried that if we had overslept we would have missed the beautiful early morning colors. Thanks to its zeal we could finally enjoy, over breakfast, the verandah's river view we had only been able to imagine the previous evening.

Banana pancakes were on offer again, and this would become a habitual company for most of our future breakfasts in Northern Laos. There are two types of banana pancakes one commonly finds in Laos: the first kind, which we got here in Nong Khiaw, was made mixing the crushed bananas with the pancake dough before frying, and it is excellent. The second type, which we were served in less meticulous eateries, was just slices of bananas served on the side of plain pancakes, and it is OK but the flavors are obviously not as well amalgamated together.

Nong Khiaw was a small village on the left bank of the Nam Ou. A few very basic wood and straw guesthouses like ours had been built around the boat piers to host travelers coming by boat. The village extended further inland, and it lived along one main street which ran parallel to the river. It was interesting to walk around because there was not much here which catered to foreign tourists; it was genuine local life which unfolded under my eyes.

I don't understand travelers who return from a trip, any trip, and say "there was nothing to do" or "there was nothing to see". If you travel to get to know the world, there is always something to see, everywhere. And to do: talk to the locals, perhaps with gestures, eat what they eat, drink with them, draw, photograph, observe, buy, give presents. Here, the real traveler, for me, is the one who, when he comes back, never, ever says that "there was nothing to do or see".

At the northern end of the main street, religious activity in a *wat* was in full swing. Some of the orange-robed monks were busy cleaning up the yard, others were awkwardly trying to pry some coconuts from a tall palm tree. Four elder monks sat cross-legged in a circle, discussing quietly who knows what. About one hundred meters outside the Wat complex, in the jungle, a young monk was kneeling down in the shade, all by himself, reading out loud a holy book of prayers which he held high. His orange shining robe stuck out of the deep green of leaves and grass all around. He was oblivious to all the noise around him, including my approach, beautifully isolated in his effort to recite his verses.

A few novices in their teens asked me to visit the temple. Scenes of inexplicable cruelty were painted on the front wall, something they described as the Buddhist hell. Women (invariably endowed with massive breasts) having their tongues cut off, men hanging lifeless at the gallows or being thrown down high cliffs. I did not know Buddhism could produce this kind of art. I'd have to read more about it.

I noticed that many of the houses used bomb casings, either whole or cut up in half, for various domestic purposes, such as support for roofs, flower pots, even just decoration. These are mostly from unexploded 1000-pound bombs dropped by American B-52s, which have been retrieved over the decades in the surrounding mountains. According to some macabre calculations, Laos has the unfortunate distinction of being the most heavily bombed country in history.

On the door of our guesthouse, as I was about to finish packing and getting ready to head back to our boat for the next leg of our cruise up the Nam Ou River, I read a poster that warned travelers as follows:

Do not buy old objects in the villages
Do not touch and do not walk across the gates of the spirits
Do not cuddle in public
Do not give incentives to beggars

The poster raised a number of issues which were very relevant to my journey. I was thinking about each of them in turn as I packed (which took only a minute or so) and walked down the treacherous muddy path to the pier where our boat was waiting (which took rather longer than one minute, even with the help of an agile local boy who offered to help with my Samsonite suitcase). So about the poster: each of the four instructions was a kind of test.

I had long been conscious of the extent of the problems caused by rich foreigners buying old personal or family objects, for example jewels or old artwork from poor people in villages. I would be tested later on, and I would pass the test.

The gates of the spirits, I had read, were very important here. It was the kind of thing, call it superstition, or whatever you want, that might make a western visitor smile. Nonetheless I believed that, when traveling, one should, out of respect, take seriously what the locals take seriously. Again I would be tested soon, and I would not pass.

Cuddling in public, well it depends, what does it mean? Kissing, hugging, holding hands? It was a bit harder to draw the line but I think, again, one should take seriously what the locals feel and better err on the side of caution than cross and red line and risk angering traditional sensitivities. Visitors could definitely wait until they were in their rooms to cuddle as much as they wanted out of the public view, though it may be hard to give up a romantic kiss at sunset on a riverbank along the Mekong. I did not kiss or cuddle so I passed this specific test.

The last warning was the most complicated. What did it mean "not to give incentive to beggars?" To give them money? Gifts? Food? Should we not give anything to people who were clearly in need just because they asked? Even if a few of them might have been fake beggars, trying to take advantage of rich tourists, was that enough to justify an end to charity for the many who actually, really did need it? I was not sure. I had a few T-shirts I did not intend to take back home, it would seem obvious to me to give them away here. Certainly someone could use them. Should I give them or keep them? Same for that extra pair of shoes I might never use again anyway, and I needed the extra space in my suitcase to take back my local purchases. I did give some stuff away, but despite the poster I am sure I passed this one particular test.

Up the river to Muang Khua

As we moved further upstream on the Nam Ou, the landscape flattened somewhat, and the steep, almost vertical cliffs made room for gentler hills. Villages along the banks become few and far between. Individual homes on stilts continued to appear, suddenly, as the boat continued to zigzag against the flow of water, dodging treacherous cross currents and various assorted floating and semi-submerged solid sources of peril. The air was still, but the brisk cruising speed of the boat produced a gentle draft which made for a deceitfully cool feeling, which promptly vanished as soon as our pirogue reached its final destination.

By mid-afternoon we were in Muang Khua, a small town on a steep section of the Nam Ou's right bank, on our left as we sailed upriver. A cement pier was almost deserted and we could comfortably disembark and unload. No sign of the van driver we had hired for the continuation of our overland trip tomorrow. OK we could worry about that later, now we needed a place to sleep.

Roberto and I left the others at the pier and went looking for a guesthouse for the night. We could find two, both pretty basic but acceptably clean and almost completely deserted. To a first approximation, I had the feeling the eleven of us had just increased the tourist population of Muang Khua by some 200 percent. We opted for a quaint guesthouse high on the riverbank, with a suspended verandah built entirely with oversize bamboo poles, some perhaps thirty centimeters in diameter, from which we could enjoy a spectacular view over the river and its left bank.

Muang Khua sat where the small River Sop Kai flows into the Nam Ou. It was the marketplace for several neighboring tribal settlements. A heart rending suspended bridge made it possible to cross the Sop Kai at a height of over 100 meters above the water, without having to descend to its riverbed, cross over by boat and climb up on the other side. Thick steel wire held the weight of the bridge, and rather loosely attached wooden planks, the size of railway sleepers, make up the usable surface. The whole structure swung eerily with the wind and rattled noisily at the passage of bikes and heavily laden carts heading for the market, but the sunset view from above was rewardingly dramatic. On the other side of the bridge a couple of paths climbed up the hills and led to several villages inhabited by different ethnic groups.

To the amusement of the locals, who did this every day, some frightened foreigners chose not to risk their lives on the bridge, safer choice but they missed quite a sight.

Dinner was at sunset, and it was made especially enjoyable by the sublime atmosphere of our terrace, except for a heavy chainsaw that the carpenter next door put to use during dinnertime – the only time of day when he had access to electricity, I guessed, so it was hard to blame him. Again lights out at 10:00 pm, some candle-light diary writing and then to sleep, whole body wet with sticky sweat, by now I was almost beginning to like it.

Suggested Reading: One Foot in Laos

Dervla Murphy had planned to trek through the high mountains of Laos, far from the country's few motor roads, but she soon encountered complications. In Laos, however, the people compensated for all that went wrong. Murphy presents her glimpse of a unique culture in this account of her journey.

Excellent travelogue peppered with questionable opinions. The author has a keen eye, is culturally curious and knows how to share her emotions through her words. Her travelogues are always informative, and this is no exception.

I have read it after my own trip to Laos and enjoyed it because she helped me see things, even retrospectively, that I had not seen, and also provided confirmation for what I did see and notice. She goes out of her way to find how people live, to get off the beaten track, to meet those whom tourists avoid and spares no effort to do so, giving up every comfort and even safety. I have done a little of what she has done, so I can admire the effort.

I do find she is too forgiving with the regime and her openly declared far left ideological bias is evident in every paragraph. I don't share it, but that does not bother me. We all have our prejudices and she has hers. I still think the travelogue part of the book is highly valuable, even unique. As for political and economic issues there are many other sources one can find and draw one's own conclusions.

She also makes frequent references to a few academic studies of Laos, but neglects many others. Perhaps she chose those that fit her theories best. In any case, again, she is free to choose her sources, and this is not an academic book, so her selectivity did not bother me. I recommend this book but it should not be the only book you read about politics, history and society in Laos.

(One Foot in Laos, Dervla Murphy, Murray, 1999.)

15. American bomb casing put to use

16. Buddhist hell in Laos

9. MUD, MONKS AND MINORITIES

Departure after the usual banana pancakes for breakfasts, I was getting a bit tired of them but it was part of the experience. Eating local food is always absolutely part of the experience of traveling, of this I am passionately convinced. So many times I have hesitated only to discover new flavors, new textures and with a little bit of reading and asking I have also learned much about a country's heritage, why do they eat what they eat.

Today we say goodbye to the river and move deep into the luxuriant hinterland, by van. It was not without some apprehension that we started our drive from Muang Khua toward the Oudomxai province. We had been warned of landslides, and were quite uncertain about how long it would take or even whether we would make it at all. We had also been reassured that work was in progress to clear the roads, but somehow that did not quite sound as reassuring as we would have wished. Anyway we were off, no choice but to move forward.

The winding road hugged spectacular mountains, climbing and descending every half an hour or so. At several points, the views were literally breathtaking, if for no other reason that the tight turns, working in concert with enormous potholes, forced the driver to put the van's wheels within centimeters of the guardrail-less narrow road, on the brink of a precipice down to the bottom of the valley, many hundreds of meters below.

We had also heard news of bandits who were active in the region, stopping cars and vans to steal anything worth anything. Foreigners with expensive cameras and potentially fat wallets were considered prime targets, so we tried to keep our eyes peeled for any sign of potential trouble. But we hardly saw anyone at all for most of the time. When we did meet another car coming in the opposite direction it was always friendly locals, and we had to cooperate very carefully to avoid hitting each other or falling over the ravine, ditch, cliff, whatever exciting feature of the landscape was at our side at any given time.

The scarab skewers of Muang Xai

This cheerless town, capital of the Oudomxai province, revealed itself to be a crossroad of cultures and races. It lies at the intersention of the main roads which lead from ventral North Laos into China to the North, Vietnam to the East and Thailand to the West.

We had dinner at a local eatery, the food was good though the mice rambling around the restaurant were somewhat less than ideal to whet our appetite. It was a small family kitchen with hearty food, each plate individually prepared for each of us by the smiling mum. Anyway, it was cheap, tasty and no one got sick, so what more could you ask for?

After dinner, I walked up the up the hill to the golden colored Pu That Pagoda until midnight. A bright full moon was rising, thanks to which I could distinctly make out the contours of the surrounding mountain ranges. All the monks were already fast asleep, and in fact not a soul was in sight. The air was perfectly still and the atmosphere in the deserted yard around the Wat exuded tranquillity and peace. I walked up the few step of the stone pyramid on which stood a simple stupa.

I sat down on the steps and spent what must have been a good hour meditating in absolute silence. The few dim lights of Muang Xai were barely a nuisance on one side, and the town noises were only just audible. By this time the full moon was gleaming over the horizon and cast a soft coat of mother-of-pearl over the Wat and the dark hillside.

I am not sure at what time I climbed down and went to sleep, but at the crack of dawn I got up and headed back to the Wat with Roberto, who was also awake ahead of schedule. The pale moon was still visible in the sky that was slowly taking a blue hue. The predictable trickle of monks dripped down the one hundred or so irregular steps which led to their dormitory, their rice baskets secured around their shoulders on their way to gather their daily offerings of rice. Muang Xai was coming to life quickly and noisily.

The market was already in full swing by the time I got there around half past six. Like the town it is part of, the market was a melting pot of cultures: Lao food was on offer side by side with Vietnamese and especially Chinese supplies. Not a few signs in fact were in Chinese. This is an important junction between the three countries, and after the end of the war it gradually came back to its full economic life. The border with China seemed to be quite open to local trade.

The more traditionally inviting stands offered familiar grilled chicken legs and wings. I was less immediately at ease with a pile of raw chicken heads, but after all they could surely make an excellent broth. Various cuts of beef and mutton were on offer, and neither buyers nor sellers seemed to pay much attention to the swarms of flies which were busy nibbling at them.

In the same meat section of the open air market, kebabs of aesthetically attractive, but gastronomically less appetizing (for me), lacquered whole scarabs were proudly displayed by their smiling butcher, who was more than happy to help me get a close look with my camera.

I was seriously tempted to buy a kebab and try a bite; after all, it was thoroughly cooked, everyone ate it here, and the rational thinker in me said I could not possibly get sick from it. I had long known that when it came to unfamiliar foreign foods an old maxim applies and always served me well: "Cook it, peel it, boil it or forget it!" However, rationality lost out to disgust and I was content with taking a few pictures. It was the first time in my travels that I refused to taste some local food. Shame on me. I made a vow never to do it again.

Desperate tiny river frogs, alive with their legs tied together with nylon strings, kicked around on top of each other in a pathetic attempt to break free from their bucket. Hundreds of freshly fished and very large river worms, a finger thick and up to twenty centimeters long, were swimming around in another bucketful of water waiting for the inevitable! In yet another bucket a whole tribe of noisily crawling live scarabs made even more of an impression on my delicate urban western senses than their kebab of grilled brethren had earlier in the day.

The landscape on the road from Muang Xai to Muang Sing was breathtakingly colorful, the ride nightmarishly grueling. The van itself was a pretty new and comfortable Toyota, and our driver was outstanding. Despite his very young age – he looked perhaps 25 and most Laotians looked older than they were – he had to have accumulated considerable experience on these roads. He was focussed like a laser beam on his driving, he was giving one hundred percent of himself, one could feel he was really into it. He drew careful trajectories on the cratered asphalt and judiciously rolled his wheels on every available square centimeter of smooth surface so as to minimize our discomfort. At times he was forced to slow down and almost come to a halt before each of the million unavoidable potholes along the road. Yet, despite all his best efforts, we averaged less than twenty kilometers per hour, and after a short while I began to feel as if shaken out of my own body. To go any faster would have meant unbearable bouncing, probable damage to our van's undercarriage and getting stuck here for a long time indeed.

Along the way, we stopped at several villages inhabited by tribal minorities of Northern Laos, including Houeita, a village of the Kmu; Kolong and Pang Thong, inhabited by the Hmong, and Namdeng, inhabited by the Lantan. It would be impossible for me to relate the details of the differences among them. What all of them had in common was that they were inhabited by ethnic minorities, very distinct from the main Lao nation. Few in these villages even spoke Lao, as we could tell because Somlit himself, our guide, had to struggle to understand and be understood.

At Namdeng I bought some small embroideries from an old lady and a few minutes later, while I was strolling around taking pictures, a young woman, perhaps in her mid-twenties, approached me and offered to sell a lovely silver necklace she was wearing. It was a typical Hmong jewel, a simple design of a circular hoop of silver, perhaps twenty centimeters in diameter and half a centimeter thick, with an opening in the front just big enough to let the thin neck of a Hmong woman slide through. At the opening, the two ends of the loop were bent backward and pressed flat to form a sort of hook on each side. I had seen similar ones in the Vientiane morning market on sale for sixty dollars and in one of Luang Prabang's chic boutiques for one hundred and twenty. With Somlit's help I gathered she wants one hundred dollars for it.

I was tempted to buy it, as it was a beautiful piece and buying it here probably guaranteed it was a true local manufacture and not a fake for tourists. However, I hesitated. First of all, I recalled the sign at the guesthouse in Nong Khiaw, which exhorted visitors not to buy old stuff from the villagers. All too often the latter sold precious family objects for a few dollars and thus quickly impoverished their village and dispersed their heritage. I did not want to do that. I asked Somlit to interpret for me and the lady said this indeed was her family's necklace. I told her she should keep it in the family, but she insisted that she was determined to sell it.

Second, the almost complete lack of communication made it difficult to understand what it was that I would be buying, what kind of silver alloy, how old, what was the artistic origin of that type of necklace, and therefore it seemed to me it just did not make much sense to take it away from the village. Did I really like that necklace? I would not be able to wear it, of course. At the moment, I did not have a wife or fiancée to gift it to, either, though of course I could keep it in reserve and possibly have a reasonable chance at impressing a lady later on in my life. Was it just a sort of trophy to be displayed upon returning home, a memento of this journey? Had I seen it in a different and less picturesque context, would I have been attracted to it anyway? Hard to say. In the end, I thanked the black clad lady for the offer but did not buy. She was a bit disappointed but smiled and went home.

I am still not sure I did the right thing. On the one hand, yes one could argue I left behind, where it belonged, a piece of Hmong art. All too often, in poor countries, visitors buy local art for pennies, and after the pennies are quickly spent by the sellers, irreparable damage is done to the country's heritage. On the other hand, the lady obviously needed or wanted the money, and therefore she probably sold the necklace to the next passing visitor, so chances are that by the time I am writing these notes it is already on the shoulders of some lady in the west or in Japan.

Also, it is not always a bad thing to trade in art, unless of course one deals in irreplaceable ancient items of historical importance. That necklace certainly did not seem to be a unique piece, more could and probably would be made in the village. Wherever it now is, the silver lace is likely to be seen and talked about and thus will contribute to make the Hmong a bit better known and appreciated, and thereby perhaps help their lot. I think if I could rewind time I would probably buy it.

The market of Muang Sing

A mellow sunset welcomed our van in Muang Sing. In the distance we could see the mountains of Yunnan province, in China. After a basic dinner, we took a walk. We passed by a disco, which consisted of an empty room with a couple of dozen bare light bulbs of different colors hanging on the walls and some sort of (to me) unidentifiable local rock music blasting mercilessly from a rudimentary but very powerful sound system. I decided I did not really need to stay to enrich my Lao sound and sights experience and left to continue my walk along the main street. I did not go far. In Muang Sing electricity was provided only in the evening between around six and ten or so. By the time I was a few hundred meters down the main street all lights went off. I could not see a thing, though the moonlight helped me retrace my steps back to the guesthouse. Time to sleep, it had been a long day!

Six o'clock in the morning and the market was already in full swing. Ladies from around the province were deployed to their negotiating positions behind tightly packed stands: tropical fruits, unidentifiable (to me) vegetables of all shapes and colors, spices, sweets, the usual suspects as far as Asian country markets go. Some clearly identifiable foodstuffs did make me wonder what kind of recipes would be prepared that evening in some of Muang Sing's homes: live beetles, whole raw pig heads, buckets of chicken paws, pig feet with hoof included.

Women from the minority Akha tribe, which inhabit most of the surrounding mountain areas, stood out for the brighter colors and adornments of their clothes as well as for their more aggressive attitude toward potential clients. They did not have fixed stands on the market floor, I was told the local Lao would not let them.

In fact, the notorious scorn, even the contempt the Akha were held was at times quite palpable around the market. Given the circumstances, the Akha had to make do by constantly walking around the aisles of the market area and approaching potential buyers. They looked like they were patrolling the area on a search and destroy mission!

The search was the easy part as they patrol the aisles between the long rows of market stands: we foreigners – the obvious sources of higher revenues for them – were obviously conspicuous and slow-moving prey. Once a target showed up on their radar screen, they quickly locked on to it and began the final approach; then, in real time, the passed on the relevant target coordinates to the rest of the wolf-pack and all moved in for the kill, surrounding us and shoving their bracelets, belts, hats et similia on to our hands. It would have been virtually impossible to make an escape, or even to break eye contact, without buying at least a trinket or two.

Which I actually did with pleasure: their embroideries, for instance, were exquisite, and their asking prices quite reasonable. One dollar bought three or four bracelets studded with cowry shells, or one belt, or a hat. Their combined use of colorful cloth, beads, mother of pearl and small shells makes for a diversified range of delicate apparel. I wondered how in the world they got cowry shells, which are harvested in the ocean, to be raw material for tribal artifacts here in the mountains. But then again cowry shells from the Indian Ocean have been used as money all over Africa since time immemorial.

This market was a photographer's gold mine. Many South East Asian markets are, but never did I see the rich assortment of different ethnic groups, each with its distinctive bodily features and tribal dresses as here in Muang Sing. The ladies obviously knew that their image was worth something to me. Most of them were quite happy to be photographed, and a few are even clearly proud to show off their elaborate dresses. They did not mind to pose but clearly expected payment.

As a general rule I do not like to pay my subjects to pose, though in this case it was possible to factor the permission to shoot into the price of some of their handicraft or produce, and that felt fine. So I came away with a few more bracelets and belts than I had anticipated or had use for, but they would make nice gifts back home and I was happy both for my photos and for having supported some local traditional artisan workshop.

In general, I do think it is important to try to support local skills, especially if the final product is genuine traditional hand-made handicraft. Maybe this would even delay the day when even this market sells plastic bracelets made in Hong Kong or Thailand. Sometimes I hesitate when it is clear that local labor is performed by children who should be in school. The problem is, if those kids were not working making trinkets, they would not be in school. They would be in the muddy street, or pushing drugs. I support any campaign to put kids in school, of course, but I do not think boycotting their products helps.

On one occasion, I improvised a curious variation on the theme of my purchase-for-photo policy. My subject was a pretty lady selling some raw vegetables, amongst which was a pile of green beans; without thinking much about it, I bought some and took my photos of the smiling vendor. I was then left with more than a handful of green beans for which I had little use in the foreseeable future. I almost returned them to the lady who had sold them to me, but I thought that might be seen as disrespectful, maybe she could think I did not appreciate her horticultural achievements, and so I walked away, camera in one hand and green beans in the other.

Then another friendly and colorful lady approached, she probably saw my awkward handling of the veggies and tried both Akha and sign language to explain something related to the beans, perhaps how to cook and eat them. She was quite an attractive subject herself, so I offered the beans to her and used sign language to try to explain that she would make a much better meal of them than I ever could, and I would let her have them in exchange for permission to take her photo. She was (understandably) a bit puzzled at first, but quickly accepted.

In the end, a few cents' worth of green beans got me not one but two distinct permissions to photograph fascinating subjects, I was satisfied and left behind two cheerful ladies, one with my money and the other with my green beans! I could only imagine the face of the husband of the second lady when he asked at dinner how much she paid for the beans and she told him of this funny western guy to whom she was trying to explain how to eat beans but was so hopeless that he gave them away in exchange for a photograph!

The only ones who resolutely turned their heads away and, at first, did not want to be photographed were some older ladies, who looked perhaps sixty to sixty-five years old – and therefore were probably in their fifties... I was told they usually refuse to pose because they think they are ugly. That was a pity, as their majestic wrinkled features were in a way the most beautiful, certainly the most interesting of all, they clearly had a story to tell and in my view were quite photogenic. In a few cases I tried sign language to explain that they were not ugly, they were beautiful, and one or two were clearly flattered, had a good laugh with one hand on their mouth (which sometimes covered teeth-less gums) and agreed to pose. I interpreted their sign language expressions to mean something like "why do you want a picture of me? I am not pretty, I am old, you should photograph some of the young girls over there" but in the end they loved the unexpected attention.

As for all the others who doggedly refused to be immortalized on my film, I respected their shyness, or desire for privacy, though I confess that I did surreptitiously take a few shots of one or two irresistible senior ladies who were not looking. OK normally one should ask, and I almost never shoot subjects who do not want to be photographed, it is one of the basic rules of courtesy for travel photographers all over the world, or at least it should be. However, candid photos are often the best, and by definition one cannot ask permission to take one. Since these ladies did not even notice I was there, I tried to persuade myself that no harm was done. I would try to push my luck a bit further in this respect at a later stage, in the hills, and will be punished for it... more on this in the pages which follow.

Around the outer limits of the market square, one Akha lady quietly approached and discretely showed me a pretty folded hat made of cotton and beads, then carefully opened to reveal an opium ball hidden inside. She repeatedly mumbled something which I did not understand but could easily guess; she would not give up easily when I hand signed that I was not interested in a smoke, and finally left me alone after a good fifteen minutes, only to approach my travel companions a few meters behind. Opium is abundant in the region, we are near the "Golden Triangle" between Thailand, Myanmar and Laos an opium growing basket since time began. It is part of the culture. I did buy an opium pipe from one of the ladies, I would bring two back home, but I never smoked them. Not interested, and certainly not worth the risk of an encounter with the local police.

It took some time to shake off the last persistent Akha ladies who chased me out of the market to sell their wares. They came all the way back to the hotel but they were not allowed on the premises. Undeterred, they sat down by the door of the verandah where food was being served and displayed all their remaining bracelets, necklaces and belts and hats on the floor. They watched assiduously while I worked away at my daily ration of banana pancakes. When I was done and set out to leave, they all got up as one and encircled me, shoving stuff in my hands and under my nose. I felt an urge to help them and buy some more of their adornments but I held back; I had already filled several of my pockets and it was clear that there would be no end to their sales pitches as long as I was within reach. So I waved them good bye, smiled, and left.

17. Akha girl selling her wares at the market

Trekking and lao lao

After the recent torrential rains, it was August after all and the monsoon season was in full swing, the way to our intended destination was blocked by high waters. We took off our shoes and socks and waded through the murky water, getting our trousers wet in spite of futile attempts to roll them up above our knees. Once safely across on the opposite bank, Somlit taught us how to insert wet tobacco in our socks so as to keep away the new threat we have to face today, as if having braved malaria-carrying mosquitoes was not enough: leeches! It was the wet season and these lovely creatures thrive in the wet mud and in rice fields.

A woman holding an infant was standing by the water. She was watching with curiosity while we waded, and we surely must have looked ridiculous for going through all that effort just to avoid getting our shoes wet and walk a few kilometers in the mud. Of course, that was easy for her to do, since she surely had done it every day of her life and she was not wearing any shoes, in or out of the water!

She was pretty and very photogenic standing with her child in her arms. As I raised my telephoto lens her amused expression turns into puzzlement. "Have you never seen nude breasts before or what? Or is there something wrong with me?" she seemed to be thinking. In fact there was nothing at all that was wrong with her, and much that was very right: she was healthy and beautiful, so was her child, and her pose by the riverbank made for a great picture.

That was what many photographers of the early XXI century are looking for: cute, politically correct, violence abhorring, environment conserving images. Not necessarily the reality of what is in front of us. If we see something unpleasant, or someone less attractive than we have been made to think by current stereotypes, we do not shoot photos, we do not even want to look. In the best of circumstances we might think of helping. How different we are from those who came here in the past.

In the good old days of the past, western explorers and conquerors would enslave or evict the locals, exterminate the wildlife, extract natural resources and otherwise exploit nature to the hilt when intruding in developing countries. And one would not call them "developing" to begin with, but rather underdeveloped, uncivilized, savage and the like.

The British poet Rudyard Kipling who, despite his popularity with children, was an avowed imperialist with few scruples, talked of "the white man's burden" when he exhorted the Americans to take over the

Philippines after the war with Spain in 1899. The first stanza of his poem tells it all:

> *Take up the White Man's burden*
> *Send forth the best ye breed*
> *Go bind your sons to exile*
> *To serve your captives' need;*
> *To wait in heavy harness*
> *On fluttered folk and wild*
> *Your new-caught, sullen peoples,*
> *Half devil and half child.*

Just thinking about colonial powers in Indochina. Over several centuries, the French of *mission civilisatrice* (civilizing mission) to justify their own imperial ambitions. The Dutch spoke of e*thische politiek,* (ethical policy), their duty to improve the lot of their colonies, nearby Indonesia first and foremost. I am not sure the Portuguese, Spanish, Belgians, Italians and Germans bothered to find a slogan, but the underlying philosophy was the same.

Even today, students in Europe are taught that yes colonialism is a thing of the past but while others just exploited the locals "our country" did a lot of good. So French kids are taught how France built schools and roads and gave the French language to the locals. Which is even true, never mind the destruction of the local culture and economic exploitation. Italians are taught how we built roads and schools in Ethiopia. Again, it is true, "la strada degli italiani" ("the Italians' road"), built in the 1930s, remained the only communication artery on the Ethiopian plateau for many decades. (There is talk that the Chinese will build another one soon.)

Post-colonial administrations, especially in Africa, have often been so corrupt and inefficient that they made one miss the imperialists. No, not really, of course, but newly independent states have a way to lose their way before people can start enjoying the benefits.

Closer to this region, the Japanese wanted other Asians to believe they were intent on building an continental "co-prosperity sphere", under Japanese leadership of course, but for the good of all Asians.

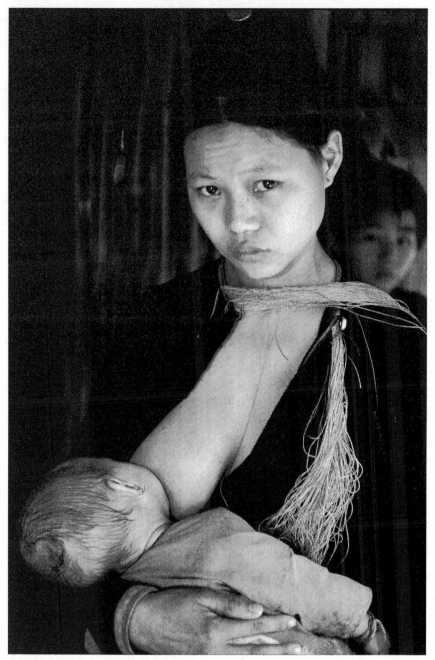

18. Village life in northern Laos

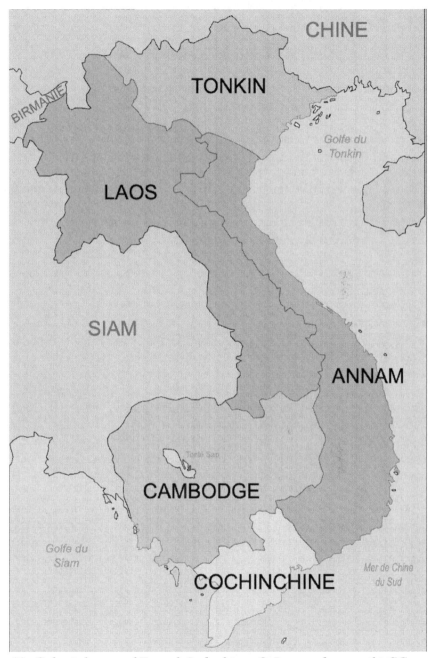

19. Colonial map of French Indochina. © Laurentleap, wiki CC

The wedding of Phouko

At the next village, called Phouko, we were in luck. In addition to the usual swarms of muddy children and skinny chicken we ran into a wedding ceremony. The feast was taking place on the upper floor of a large house on stilts. We were cordially invited to join in. The extent to which we could communicate was limited, to put it mildly, and even Somlit was at a loss to move beyond very basic concepts with the Akha. However, it was unmistakably clear that we were welcome. Several fires were lit inside the house, which initially made me a bit uneasy as the wood, wicker and straw the building was made of, as well as every piece of furniture inside, was supremely inflammable and could have been ignited by the smallest of stray sparks. Once again, I entrusted my life to the laws of probability, and decided it was very unlikely a fire would start just today.

But our hosts, while under the influence of lao lao, looked as if they knew what they were doing. It was not difficult to fall under the influence of lao lao, as I would personally experience on a number of jolly occasions during this trip.

Lao lao is a distilled spirit made of rice. Contrary to what the identical transliteration into Latin letters might suggest, the name is not the same word repeated twice, but two different words pronounced with different tones: the first lao means alcohol and is pronounced with a low-falling tone, while the second lao means Laotian and is pronounced with a rising tone. It is similar to what the Chinese refer to as *jiu*, rice whisky, and it offers a rather bland taste to the palate but a high alcohol content, I would say 40+ by volume. It is often paired very well with the coconut-based recipes of the Laotian cuisine, though most commonly it is consumed during festive occasions.

All the elderly women were sitting around one of the fires, in one corner. Most wore elaborate ornaments, were merrily chatting away among themselves and hardly paid any attention to us, or to their men for that matter. Some younger women stood on one side with the bride, and were a bit shy when I approached them. After a few vain attempts I persuaded a few to pose for me, and then they were clearly pleased to do so. From the outset I had the definite impression that they really wanted to be photographed but perhaps conventional Akha modesty, or the presence of their elders, dictated that they hide and play timid at first.

The senior men were drinking tea and lao lao around their own fire. They directed all of us guests (men and women) toward the men's fire and using sign language explained that custom had it that each of us was expected to drink one shot of lao lao in one gulp, followed by a cup of tea, in order to be formally admitted to partake of the wedding. At around eleven o'clock in the morning, and with an empty stomach, a glassful of lao lao – their "shot" glass was not like those small ones we use for vodka shot, but rather closer to the size of a cup of tea – did not go down unnoticed, especially not with temperatures close to 40° centigrade in the sun.

After the first shot I began to sweat even more profusely than I already was, but what the heck, my shirt could not get any more soaked than it already was. In fact at that point it was also the photo-vest which I wore over my shirt that was darkening as salty perspiration worked its way outward to evaporate and leave a white salty patina all over. I admit that for my second shot I cheated, and took advantage of the confusion all around to sip it in stages and sneak some tea in between...

It was a highly emotional experience to be part of this wedding ceremony. It was one occasion in which it seemed that the language barrier collapsed, perhaps under the repeated assaults of lao lao mega-shots, or perhaps because the spiritual meanings of wedding ceremonies have much in common the world over. Yet, I was thinking as I watched the scened of joy all around, what would be the reaction at your average wedding in Europe, or in America, if a dozen perfect strangers from an unknown country all dressed in funny exotic clothes would suddenly pop up uninvited, cameras in hand, strobe lights flashing and no gifts for either bride or groom!

Well, they actually did take care of the latter. After we were done drinking, we were accompanied down the stilts to the adjacent yard, where newlyweds displayed themselves to the whole village. Then someone approached Somlit and asked for a few thousand kips' offering to the couple. Fair enough, that would be our wedding gift.

The spirits of Namdat's gate

We were slowed down at the Akha village of Pakha by leeches which got into Paola's shoes. We had been warned they were omnipresent here, they crawled into shoes, dropped from trees into shirt collars and stopped at nothing to suck a visitor's blood. Some (me included) had followed Somlit's advice and put tobacco inside our socks, apparently the aroma is not appreciated by leeches. Well, I am not sure if it was because of that, most of us were safe except for poor Paola. Not a big deal really. It was enough to take off her shoes and socks and put the flame of a lighter next to the beast and it fell off to the ground.

At Namdat, the next Akha village on our trekking itinerary, I learned a lesson. I took a photo of a bare breasted lady nursing an infant by a water fountain. She made it abundantly clear that she did not want to be photographed, but I shot one frame anyway. Barbara reprimanded me severely, "Do you think they have no rights to privacy just because they are tribal peoples?"

She was right, no question about it, and I was wrong, but it was such a perfect shot, the light was right, the lady was pretty, her baby even prettier and the fountain added a perfect context, so I had to take that photograph. I knew I had done something wrong, but I also tried to persuade myself that it was not really a mortal sin, just a photo which would never appear on any commercial publication, what harm could this possibly do to the pretty lady, or to her son for that matter, etc but I could not really come up with a good excuse. Anyway, the photo was taken and it was too late now to do anything about it, ...or so I thought.

At that point I noticed we were leaving the Namdat village and I was walking past the "Gate of the Spirits", the sacred wooden frame which one often finds at the outskirts of many Akha villages in Northern Laos. The gate protects the village from the spirits and if it is violated they must be appeased with expensive animal sacrifices. I remembered the poster at the guesthouse in Nun-Khiaw which expressly warned not to touch or walk through these gates, and kept well clear of it.

I did it out of respect because, of course, I did not believe in ghosts and spirits then as I do not now.

Somlit had also told us stories of some northern European tourists who had made fun of the gate, touching it and nonchalantly walking through. They had been seen by some villager who called for the chief, who was not amused. The tourists were taken to a home and detained and were not released until the agreed to pay for several farm animals to be slaughtered and offered to appease the spirits.

As it happened, at that point I noticed that frame of the lady at the fountain was the last one in my roll of Fuji Velvia. I pushed the rewind button and the camera began rewinding the film while I was getting ready to load a fresh roll. I looked up to the gate one more time and at that very moment my camera's rewinding motor screeched to a halt and jammed. It had never, ever happened to me before, nor has it ever happened since. I shook the camera, pushed different buttons, tried to reset it, yelled at it, but it just refused to cooperate. The only thing left to do was to open the camera's back and undo the jam by hand.

That, of course, meant that the picture of the lady at the fountain would surely be lost, and with it probably also those of the Yao ladies from the previous village. In the end I managed to unjam the camera by hand, put in a fresh roll and took a couple of shots of the Gate of the Spirits, keeping a careful distance just in case. The village gate, for the Akha, separates the safe human space, protecting the villagers from the spirits who emerge from the underworld looking for souls to eat. I could not help but thinking that the spirits had punished me for my overbearing attitude toward the lady at the fountain.

But, of course, I repeated to myself that I did not believe in ghosts and spirits.

Suggested Reading: Meet the Akhas

A comprehensive introduction to the Akha hill tribals of Northern Thailand and their way of life includes a language section to enable you to talk to your hosts.

The Akha of Thailand, as well as those of China, are the same ethnic group as those we met in Laos. Their history and culture do not follow the political borders of the map. Goodman writes one of the few accounts of the Akha, an ethnic group whose lands straddle Thailand, Laos and China. Many interesting details ontheir culture in this little book, and good photographs. Hope for a reprint as it is now impossible to find.

(Meet the Akha, by Jim Goodman, White Lotus, Bangkok, 1996.)

Minorities in Laos according to national Census of 1995				
Minority	Villages	Population	Houses	Temples
Akha	68	11.000	2300	0
Lua	26	6.000	1200	18
Kmu	1	81	19	0
Hmong	3	2000	300	0
Toi Nema	5	2000	300	0

The courtesans of Luang Namtha

Another town which was much destroyed by US bombing and has now found a new lease on life from tourism and trade with China. Lots of advertising boards in Chinese here, and several hotels and restaurants were owned by Chinese interests; Chinese products, including food, was widely available. We were unmistakably very, very close to China...

I spotted a notice on the wall of our guesthouse rooms in Laotian and English. Glued on the wooden partition was an unusual collection of threats and warnings, conveying a number of attitudes and prescriptions, ranging from a rather usual disclaimer (not to leave your valuables in the room), to the more original one which read:

**IT IS FORBIDDEN TO BRING
SEXUAL GIRLS (COURTESANS)
INTO YOUR ROOM,
ILLEGAL THINGS OR DRUGS
OR PLAY ANY GAMBLING SUCH AS CARDS
OR ANY OTHER BAD THINGS**

I had heard and read that prostitution was becoming widespread in Laos, as well as Cambodia, especially as Thailand had begun to crack down on child prostitution under international pressure.

It was also a question of money: according to numerous reports, commercial sex in Thailand was getting more and more expensive, while a young girl, maybe a virgin, even a minor, in Laos or Cambodia could obviously be had at a fraction of the price.

Dinner at a nondescript eatery illuminated by cool neon lamps. We joined a few locals who were munching away some dishes which I am not able to describe but smelled very good, sweet and sour, some kind of meat for sure. We ordered the same by pointing them to the waiter. Drink was beer and tea, and the atmosphere was altogether quiet and pleasant despite a big rat, or two, that every now and then zapped across the wooden beams that were holding the roof of the building.

Back to the hotel room and in bed early, we did not bring any sexual girls (courtesans), illegal things or drugs. Kind of boring when I think back to that night, but we did not even play any gambling such as cards or any other bad things. We just hit the sack and fell asleep. Tomorrow was going to be another long day.

Back to Luang Prabang

Got up early to go and see the monks climb up to a nearby pagoda, that was sitting smack on top of a small hill, for prayers before breakfast. Maybe a dozen or so of them, in their early twenties or younger, wrapped in their bright orange robes and smiling politely. I did not want to disturb them, it was all so quiet, so I asked permission to take a few photos, which they allowed with joy, and descended back down for my own breakfast.

Today long transfer to Luang Prabang. A bumpy ride in the luxuriant forests of northern Laos. Always lively with people and herds. Never monotonous. Along the way a reminder of Europe: at a village that seems in pretty good shape we saw a big sign with a faded blue flag with the unmistakable circle of 12 stars of the European Union, which has funded development projects in the area.

The village allowed us some interesting time travel. Houses made of wooden poles and mud bricks; pigs and chicken roaming free. Many women around, young women most of whom carried a child on their back. Some older children played in the mud or in the watering tanks for the animals. They were all dressed in simple rags, and inevitably wore some colorful jewels. Their exposed upper body and breasts revealed toned muscles and a soft brown skin.

When we arrived at Luang Prabang we went straight to sleep at the same guesthouse as the last time, the French-speaking lady was waiting for us. Felt a bit like home after the adventure of the last few days.

In fact it felt a lot like home: clean beds, varied food presented on proper plates, fans, bicycles. And being able to speak French and understand each other without using hand gestures. It could have been English, or Italian for me, but in the past few weeks, with the notable exception of Somlit, I had hardly been able to use any language at all with the Laotians we had met.

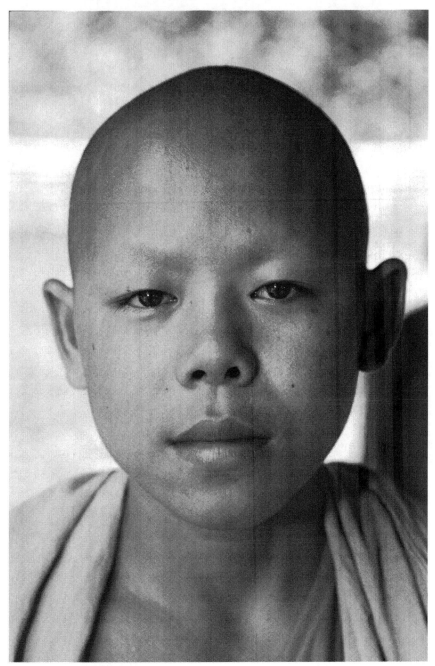

20. Buddhist novice

21. Daily life in a village

10. BYE-BYE INDOCHINA

I was sitting in a window seat in the forward section of the plane, on the left hand side of the aisle and just forward of the big eight-bladed propeller. Ever since I began traveling by air I have always asked for window seats, even if it was often not the most comfortable. I have always been curious to begin the discovery of a new trip already in flight; of course, most of the time the view from outside the plane is nothing to write home about, but once in a while a good combination of weather, landscape and flight trajectory rewards my perseverance. The last glimpse of Laos I was given to enjoy could not have been a more appropriate one.

The late afternoon sun was shining and casting a warm, gentle light over the jungle. After take-off, the plane made an almost completely full circle before settling on its south-westerly course toward Bangkok. As it looped around Luang Prabang's peninsula, the Mekong showed its majestic elegance one last time, its sinuous turns seemed to wave us off. I could easily make out the Pak Ou Caves and the suburbs of Luang Prabang, from where we had cruised on our way to Nong Khiaw. The narrower Nam Ou river appeared as well, to the north, with its steep rocky cliffs punctuating its last leg before it feeds into the big brother Mekong.

The turboprop might as well have been a spacecraft, or a time machine, because balmy Luang Prabang, muddy Pakse or run-down Vientiane do not belong to the same planet, nor to the same era, as Bangkok. Stepping out of the airplane one had the definite impression of having fast-forwarded back into the XXI century.

I had a couple of days in Bangkok before heading out of Indochina. The name means the "city of angels" and for some years it had been twinned, guess what, with Los Angeles in California!

Bangkok was a bustling metropolis, full of life and activity, be it economic, cultural or entertainment. The "emerging" Thailand had definitely emerged! The best way around, I find, is by boat, though I have had fun taking a few tuk-tuk rides in the hectic traffic. Tuk-tuks are tricycles powered by a two-stroke engine, they resemble Piaggio's "Ape" used for transport everywhere in India and derived from an Italian design of the 1940s. It's cheap and cheerful, though not necessarily the safest way to navigate Bangkok traffic.

Then there were the ferries along the river, also fast and cheap and much safer. Whenever possible I always moved around by ferry in Bangkok. One afternoon I visited the Jim Thompson house. He was an American secret service agent who worked here in WW II and stayed afterwards. In the fifties he started collecting artifacts from old Thai homes and assembled what is perhaps the most valuable collection at his home. This is now the best example of traditional Thai home available, and since his mysterious disappearance in 1967 it has become a museum. There is also a classy shop with fine silk products. A most interesting and serene place.

One evening I decided to go to the famous *Oriental Hotel* for dinner and a dance show. I could reach the hotel by means of a free boat shuttle that crosses the river at regular intervals. The food was great and the show well arranged. Around me mostly well-to-do Thai patrons, though quite a few tourists contributed to fill the hall.

Tiziano Terzani repeatedly stayed here in the 1970s when he was reporting on Cambodia's horrors. So did many other famous people over the last few decades, when Thailand was still an "emerging" economy and this was the only luxury hotel in town.

My journey was really over.

On my next flight out, to the United States, I was handed a form I needed to fill out to enter the country. My Italian passport allowed me to get in without a visa, but everyone needed to fill out this form.

The visa waiver form asked whether the passport holder seeking to enter the United States was a member of the Nazi party. Fair question, even more than half a century after the end of the Holocaust Americans want to know whether a perpetrator of such heinous crimes was about to enter their country. Until recently the same form used to ask whether one was, or had been, a communist.

I could not help think however why the United States, or any other country for that matter, did not bother to ask whether a visitor was ever part of Pol Pot's regime, responsible for what was, in relative terms, an even more comprehensive genocide than the Holocaust.

But if the United States did raise such a question on its visa form, some could then ask embarrassing questions, such as why the Americans (together with most other western European countries and Communist China) continued to support Pol Pot's claim to the Cambodian seat at the United Nations even after their crimes became widely known in the 1980s.

The answer was easy, of course: the successors of Pol Pot were pro-Vietnamese, and Vietnam was pro-Soviet and that was still the time of the Cold War. A perfectly justifiable political argument, but one which it was easier not to have to make.

Lettura consigliata (italiano): Caduti dal Muro

C'era una volta il Muro e sembrava dovesse esarci per sempre. Poi però il Muro si sbriciolò e con esso crollò un impero che da Berlino arrivava al Pacifico. Di colpo tramontò il "sole dell'avvenire", sparirono mappe geografiche, bandiere, nomenclature. Ma cosa ne è stato di quei paesi?

Per capirlo serve un viaggio lento, zaino in spalla e treno attraverso due continenti, dall'Europa orientale alla Russia, dalla Cina al Vietnam, dalla Cambogia ai Tibet. Un viaggio e un dialogo tra due scrittori divisi dall'anagrafe e dalle parabole della politica ma uniti dalla leggerezza e dalla fame di nuovi orizzonti. (dalla quarta di copertina)

Riflessioni di viaggio (di Tito) e di storia (di entrambi) nelle terre che erano governate da regimi comunisti fino alla fine degli anni 80 del XX secolo. Il viaggio di Tito è occasione di ricordare un mondo che non esiste più, un mondo nel quale gli autori avevano creduto, assieme a milioni di idealisti in occidente che non avevano visto quello che veramente succedeva al di là del muro. Si impara molto leggendo questo libro, soprattutto chi non è stato in quei luoghi, in quei tempi.

Prosa fluida, in certi punti del libro sembra di essere con loro, sia nel luoghi, sia nei tempi storici richiamati alla memoria. Unica piccola pecca: se abbondano le critiche a quei comunisti che hanno "perso" (URSS, Europa orientale) manca una critica dei crimini commessi da quei comunisti che hanno "vinto", specialmente quelli del Vietnam, durante la guerra contro l'invasore americano. Se i crimini americani sono giustamente evidenziati, non altrettanto lo sono quelli commessi dai nord vietnamiti e Viet Cong. Consiglio di leggere Oriana Fallaci per colmare la lacuna, specialmente il suo libro "Saigon e Così Sia" e anche "Niente e Così Sia").

(Caduti dal Muro, di Tito Barbini e Paolo Ciampi, Vallecchi, 2009.)

Lettura consigliata (italiano): Fantasmi

La Cambogia è stato uno dei grandi amori di Tiziano Terzani. La storia di questo piccolo regno, che custodisce al suo interno i misteriosi templi di Angkor, divenne per lui emblematica della storia dei paesi dell'Asia travolti nel corso del XX secolo dai giochi delle grandi potenze (USA, Cina, URSS). Terzani visitò più volte il Paese tra il 1972 e il 1994, divenne amico del suo re e nemico indignato degli assassini khmer rossi, per denunciare infine come ipocrita e immorale anche l'operato di pace da parte delle Nazioni Unite,

Il libro, fondato sui reportage di Terzani dalla Cambogia, contiene anche il racconto scritto in prima persona della sua cattura da parte di combattenti ragazzini, dell'attimo in cui si salvò la vita con una risata – come amava raccontare – e circa cinquanta fotografie originali, scattate spesso da lui stesso.

Terzani ci racconta gli orrori della Cambogia dei Khmer Rossi. In realtà ci racconta dei racconti che ha ascoltato, perché in quel periodo lui, come tutti i corrispondenti stranieri, in Cambogia non poteva entrarci.

Ciononostante il libro è una miniera d'oro di informazioni, e le riflessioni che Terzani ci propone molti anni dopo la fine del regime lo sono ancora di più.

Unica pecca, che ricorre negli scritti di Terzani sull'Indocina, è il persistente atteggiamento anti-americano e anti-modernità. Lui riconosce, con grande onestà intellettuale, di essersi sbagliato sui Khmer Rossi, ma negli anni settanta sembrava cercare sempre un motivo per dubitare delle denunce che urlavano gli scampati. Mentre ogni occasione è buona per accusare gli americani, che pure di colpe ne hanno avute tante, o anche i giapponesi, per il loro imperialismo economico.

Poi si rammarica che anonimi palazzi abbiano preso il posto delle catapecchie, ma non pensa che anche ai cambogiani possano servire acqua corrente e elettricità. Insomma una testimonianza appassionata e consigliata, ma viziata da un pregiudizio ideologico di fondo.

(Fantasmi: Dispacci dalla Cambogia, di Tiziano Terzani, Bompiani, 2008.)

22. Good-bye Mekong!

CHRONOLOGY

IX century AD to 1431

Khmer kingdom, Angkor flourishes as the capital city.

1431
Capital is moved to Phnom Penh

1887
Following a war with China, France establishes a colony in Vietnam (Tonkin in the north, Annam in the center and Cochinchina in the south) and Cambodia.

1893
After defeating Thailand in a brief war, France established a colony in Laos.

1941
Norodom Sihanouk becomes king of Cambodia for the first time.

1940-1944
French Vichy forces retain control of Indochinese colonies with Japan's acquiescence.

1944

French Vichy forces are defeated by Japan and surrender colonies.

1945
France takes back its Indochinese colonies from Japan.

1954
The French are decisively defeated by the Vietnamese at Dien Bien Phu and leave Indochina.

Cambodia becomes an independent country.

Laos becomes an independent country.

1960s
North Vietnamese fighters infiltrate Cambodia and Laos to establish the "Ho Chi Minh trail" of military supplies and guerrilla forces to fight in South Vietnam.

1964-1973
United States bombs Laos to stop supplies going through the "Ho Chi Minh trail" and to weaken Laotian communist forces.

1970
Monarchy abolished in Cambodia, republic established.

1969-1970
US president Nixon bombs officially neutral Cambodia to suppress "Ho Chi Minh trail" of supplies from North Vietnam.

April 1975
The Khmer Rouge take Phnom Penh, begin governing Cambodia, which they rename "Democratic Kampuchea".

April 1975
The Americans complete evacuation from Saigon. North Vietnamese forces take over the whole country.

January 1979
Vietnam invades Cambodia. Khmer Rouge are overthrown, run to the jungle and continue guerrilla warfare.

1979-1990
The USA, China, and most western countries continue to recognize the Khmer Rouge as the legitimate representatives of Cambodia at the United Nations. Soviet Union and its allies recognize new government installed by Vietnam.

1993
Monarchy restored in Cambodia with Norodom Sihanouk as king.

1998
Pol Pot dies a prisoner of his former subordinate commanders in the west of Cambodia.

2010
Comrade Duch, the man in charge of S-21, is sentenced to 35 years, increased to life imprisonment in 2012. He dies in 2020.

2012
King Norodom Sihanouk dies. His son Norodom Sihamoni is the new king.

ABOUT THE AUTHOR

Marco was born in Rome in a Year of the Pig of the Chinese calendar.

He lived for a while in eternal city, where he was a program manager at the Istituto Affari Internazionali and contributed to the Enciclopedia Treccani. Study and work then took him to the States, where he received a Ph.D. in strategic studies from M.I.T.; to Belgium, where he worked as an international civil servant at NATO; and finally to London, where he shares his enthusiasm for this city with his Chinese wife. She, too, was born in the year of the pig, they were clearly meant for each other.

He is a curious traveler, and likes to try food from all over the world at least once, though he declined to taste grilled skewers of scarabs in Laos. However, he is extremely selective with wines, especially after he graduated as a professional sommelier.

In addition to wine and travel, Marco loves cooking, classical music, underwater photography and cool jazz, not necessarily in that order.

He writes and lectures on cruise ships about travel, international affairs and wine. His books are available on Amazon in Italian and English.

Blog www.marcocarnovale.com.

Instagram: @world.wise.wines for his wine pairings and @carno.polo for his travels.

23. Author hiking in the Lao countryside

INDEX

Printed in Great Britain
by Amazon